WINNING THE
INFORMATION
SYSTEMS GAME

X/KEL/587

"Winning The Information Systems Game"

Hudsons Bookshops

A Division of Pentos Bookselling Group Ltd

Dear Sir,

Above title   @   £10.35
Postage & Packing
                @   £0.75
Amount Paid @   £9.73
<u>BALANCE TO PAY   £1.37</u>

Yours faithfully,
X-Orders Dept.

with compliments

116 New Street, Birmingham B2 4JJ, England
Telephone: 021-643 8311

WINNING THE INFORMATION SYSTEMS GAME

Nelson T. Dinerstein
Associate Professor of Computer Science
Utah State University

Kogan
Page

First published in the US in 1985 by
Dow Jones-Irwin, Homewood, Illinois.

Copyright © Nelson T Dinerstein 1985

This edition first published in Great Britain in 1987
by Kogan Page Limited, 120 Pentonville Road,
London N1 9JN, by arrangement with Dow Jones-Irwin.

New material copyright © Kogan Page Limited 1987

This publication is designed to provide accurate and
authoritative information in regard to the subject matter
covered. It is sold with the understanding that the publisher
is not engaged in rendering legal, accounting, or other
professional service. If legal advice or other expert
assistance is required, the services of a competent
professional person should be sought.

British Library Cataloguing-in-Publication Data

Dinerstein, Nelson T.
  Winning the information systems game: a manager's
  survival guide.
  1. Management information systems
  I. Title
  658.4'038   T58.6

  ISBN 1-85091-322-6

Printed and bound in Great Britain by
Mackays of Chatham Ltd, Kent

PREFACE

Ever since the advent of the computer, middle managers have been concerned that they would be replaced by computers. The time has come to face the facts: middle managers are not replaced by computers—they are replaced by people that know how to use computers to their own advantage.

Success in the business environment is not measured in how well you do your current job but in how high you climb the promotion ladder. Promotion decisions are usually based on the image you project to your superiors. If your superiors feel you can handle the new job better than other candidates, then you'll get it. This means that you need to be visible within the organization and have a reputation for getting the job done.

This book will teach you how to use the computer to get ahead. Instead of avoiding the computer because you think of it as a potential enemy, you will learn to use the computer to make a name for yourself in your organization. It will become a major tool on your pathway to success.

Many of the techniques for success that are presented in this book have been used by the author or by middle managers that the author has observed. Not every technique will be successful for all middle managers in all circumstances. As you read this book, identify those techniques that you would like to use and incorporate them into your plan for success.

Nelson T. Dinerstein

CONTENTS

1. Introduction   1

2. The Role of the Middle Manager
in the Organization   7

3. Standing out
in the Organization   17

4. A Primer on
Information Systems   33

5. A Primer on the
Technical Abilities of
the Software Technician   55

6. Software Development Systems   87

7. The New Information System:
Part I   117

8. The New Information System:
Part II   131

9. Creative Approaches   145

10. A Case Study   165

11. Packaging Proposals
to Higher Management   177

12. Putting It All Together   191

Glossary   207

References   215

Index   217

CHAPTER 1

Introduction

You are a manager because you have the education, training, and ability to be one. You have been chosen to be a manager because others have confidence in your abilities to get the job done. For a number of years, the middle manager has been viewed as someone who had little or no training in the use of computers and was therefore afraid of them. The difficulty with computers has not been that they really were too difficult to understand, but that managers were convinced that they were too difficult to understand, both by themselves and by the technical staff. Your selection as a manager indicates that you are competent, intelligent, and a problem solver. Since the computer is nothing more than a tool for solving problems, you can learn to use this tool just like you learned to use the standard tools of your current job. After all, you certainly didn't know everything about your current job before you started it, did you?

> You can learn to use the computer as a tool to get the job done.

It is important to note here that you must stand out from the crowd to get ahead. It just isn't enough to do your job well. You must also gain recognition for your ability to face and handle new problems. One of the distinguishing characteristics of upper management is the ability to recognize both problems and opportunities. The successful high-level manager has the ability to see through to the heart of the problem, evaluate its potentials for success and failure, formulate a plan to achieve a notable success, and bring the resources to bear to accomplish the plan. In order to show high-level management that you have the qualifications to become a high-level manager, you must demonstrate the ability to perform these same tasks. It is not just a matter of doing your current job as expected. You must do it better than anyone expected, and you must do it significantly better than others who do the same type of job. The main purpose of this book is to teach you how to use the computer in an innovative manner, helping you to do your job better than expected by your superiors.

Movement to an upper-management position does not come just from doing your current job well, but by demonstrating that you have the ability to innovate and solve unusual problems.

Your organization undoubtedly uses computers. A considerable amount of time and money has been invested by your organization in the construction of a computerized information system. You must learn to use this information system to the best of your ability and for your own purposes, so that you can reduce the amount of time that you currently spend doing your job.

Use your organization's information system in an innovative manner to reduce the amount of time you spend doing your job.

Unfortunately, no organizational information system can be all things to all people. Very often, the reports that you receive have been designed by someone else, so they may have any or all of the following defects:

1. They are hard to read,
2. They contain little or no useful information,
3. They are too late to be useful,
4. The information that they contain is unreliable, and/or
5. They don't give you the information you need to do your job the way that you want to.

The last item (5) is critical. In order to advance to a high-level management position, you must not perform your job the same way that everybody else does. You must perform it so that you stand out and become visible within the organization. Doing your job in the same manner that others do it just makes you one of the pack. It does not demonstrate either your initiative or problem-solving ability.

The organizational information system is designed to help you do your job in the same manner that everyone else does it. You must learn to use it in an innovative manner, not in the same way that everyone else uses it.

First you must learn to use the organizational information system to the best of your advantage, and then you must start your own private information system. While the organizational information system is under the control of others in the organization, your private information system will be completely under your own control. The purpose of having a private (computerized) information system will be to provide you with the precise information that you need to do your job in the manner that you wish. Organizational information systems are notorious for providing mediocre levels of information and for being difficult to change. You may have a new idea that you wish to try out, but if you are not a high-level manager you will find that changes are quite difficult to bring about. Do not count on being able to get the technical staff to modify or enhance the organizational information system just to meet your needs.

Use a private information system to provide you with the information that you cannot get from the organizational information system.

Analysts and programmers that work for other departments, like the information systems department, are usually scheduled several months in advance. If you submit a request for analysis and programming services to the information systems department, you are usually told each of the following:

1. There will be a delay before your work can be started, since analysts and programmers are not available,
2. It will be necessary for you to obtain permission to make the desired changes, and
3. You will need to allocate a considerable amount of money for the project.

You may even be told that you do not have the authority to request any changes in the information system. A direct rejection of your request may be made by returning the request itself with the rejection attached. An indirect rejection may take the form of an impossible schedule.

A few years ago, I did some consulting work for a large bank in California. The personnel department of the bank had received a request from the federal government to provide a report showing the number of people in various minority groups employed by the bank. The report was to appear in two parts:

1. For each branch bank location, a count of the employees in each minority group, and
2. For each minority group, a listing of the branch banks where people from that group were employed.

The task of providing such a report was quite simple and did not require unusual resources. When the personnel department requested programming support for the project (now remember that the bank had to supply the report to the federal government), they were told that it would take two to three years before a programmer would be free for the project. The personnel department then asked if one of the members of their own staff could write the program himself, so that they would not have to wait for two or three years. Permission was granted for the personnel department to do their own programming. The attempt to use the organizational information system was terminated when the personnel department found out that their priority for running programs on the organization's computer was so low that approximately three months would elapse between the time that the program was first submitted and the time that the program was run. If it took only three tries for the personnel staff member to write a program that worked correctly, at least nine months would elapse before the report could be produced.

The development of a private information system is easier than you might think. Remember: A private information system is just another tool to help you do your job as you envision that it should be done. You already have a number of ideas concerning the information that you would like to have! It is only necessary to put these ideas to work.

> You already have a number of ideas on how to do your job better.

It is appropriate to give you a word of caution. When you first build your own private information system, don't attempt to do everything that you can think of. Carefully select the most important projects, i.e., those that have the greatest potential for advancing you to a position of high-level management. You should also be careful not to attempt to automate every part of the project. The best projects are those that have a reasonable balance between manual and automated (computer-assisted) procedures. You, not the computer, are the problem solver. The computer is merely a tool to help you discover the existence of problems, manage large volumes of data, and implement your solutions. It is true that computers can be used in a wide variety of situations, but we will focus on the use of the computer to help you to do each of the following:

1. Do your current job better,
2. Save a significant amount of money in your current job, and/or
3. Provide a service to high-level management that they need but do not currently receive.

Don't try to do too much with your private information system. Focus your energies on one or two really good projects. Automate those procedures that will help you the most, but do not try to automate everything.

In the following chapters, we will examine each of the following topics:

1. The traditional role of the middle manager.
2. A nontraditional viewpoint of the role of the middle manager.
3. The fundamentals of information systems.
4. How to use the organization's information system to your best advantage.
5. How to create and use your own private information system in a cost effective manner.
6. Suggestions on how to use both the organization's information system and your own private information system in a creative (innovative) manner.
7. How to package your proposals to high-level management.

CHAPTER 2

The Role of the Middle Manager in the Organization

2.1 The Traditional Role

Low-level management (the supervisor) has responsibility for the immediate supervision of a number of employees. This manager has the responsibility to see that:

1. The workers start and stop work at the expected times,
2. The conduct of the workers is appropriate during working hours,
3. The workers are properly trained,
4. The quality of the work performed by the workers is within the expected range, and
5. Applicable organizational policies are carried out.

High-level management has each of the following responsibilities:

1. Setting organizational goals,
2. Development of plans to accomplish organizational goals,
3. Guidance of a number of departments to ensure that plans are followed and that goals are achieved,
4. Acquisition of key personnel, and
5. Overseeing finances.

The middle manager is not only between the low-level manager (the supervisor) and the high-level manager in terms of the authority structure of the organization but is also between them in terms of job responsibilities. The middle manager:

1. Supervises a number of employees, some of whom may be managers or supervisors themselves,
2. Sets departmental goals in accordance with organizational goals,
3. Develops plans and budgets to help the department achieve these goals,
4. Determines departmental policies, and
5. Monitors daily activities to ensure that plans are carried out.

High-level management often derives a set of goals for each department. The manager of each of these departments is then expected to set departmental goals and develop plans and budgets that will directly lead to the goals set for the department by high-level management. Thus, from the traditional viewpoint, the middle manager is either expected to implement the plans made by higher management or to develop plans to meet the goals established by high-level management, rather than to develop plans independently. Therefore, the traditional role of the middle manager does not encourage innovation. The middle manager is viewed by upper management as a high-level supervisor, someone who has the ability to carry out assigned tasks.

> The traditional role of the middle manager does not encourage innovation. In fact, the traditional viewpoint of the middle manager may actually discourage innovation.

2.2 The Nontraditional Role

If you wish to move into high-level management, you must identify and succeed in the responsibilities of middle management that are most closely associated with the responsibilities of higher management. You must demonstrate not only that you can do all of the assigned tasks, but you must also demonstrate that you have the qualities necessary for higher-level management.

> You must succeed in those parts of your job that are most closely associated with the responsibilities of high-level management.

It is not necessary to work long hours in an attempt to impress people with your dedication.

A number of years ago I worked for someone who wanted me out of the office each evening by 5 P.M., unless there was a *real* emergency. He felt that the amount of work on my desk the following morning would be the same, no matter how many hours I put in the previous evening. I have thought of this advice a number of times since then, and have come to the following conclusions. People work better when they are fresh and alert. If you attempt to solve problems when you are tired (after you have already put in eight or so hours), then the quality of your work deteriorates and you spend a large number of hours without any good result.

Work smart, not hard. Instead of using all of your energy and time trying to impress someone with your dedication, impress someone with your abilities. In particular, demonstrate that you have each of the following characteristics:

1. A Fundamental Understanding of Your Environment

Show that you understand your work environment. This includes, but is not limited to, a knowledge of:

A. The people that you work with and for,
B. The people that work for you,
C. Organizational and departmental goals, plans, policies, and procedures,
D. The primary function of your department,
E. The various functions of your organization, and
F. The role of your department in the organization.

2. Intelligence

There is no substitute for intelligence. Demonstrate that you can recognize unusual problems, plan a way to solve the problem, and then implement your solution. Your plan should be to show that you have the basic intelligence, persistence, and ability not only to do your job, but also to move into high-level management. Do not try to give the impression of being brilliant, since many people try to avoid associating with others who appear to be considerably more intelligent than they themselves are.

3. Flexibility

Be able to change your way of doing things. Be able to recognize changes, choose new approaches to problem solving, and implement new plans. Flexibility is required when there is a change in the environment, forcing you to respond to the change. You can also apply your flexibility to perform better even when there is no change in the environment. Examine the way in which tasks are performed in your department. Don't be bound to traditional approaches if you feel that a different approach will bring about significant improvements.

4. The Ability to Get the Job Done

Be careful here. This does not mean that you must do the job all by yourself. You must demonstrate that you have the ability to use the available resources, including the people who work with and for you, to accomplish the assigned task. When you have accomplished the task, the people who did it for you must feel good about their role in accomplishing the task. You must not alienate those who work with and for you. Making use of the available resources to do the job better or to provide new services is important, since it does not involve allocation of new resources. High-level management is always looking for ways to bring about improvement, but the most impressive ways are those that do not require the allocation of additional resources.

5. Capacity for Innovation

The capacity for innovation is the desire and ability to bring new and different tools and problem-solving techniques to bear on both new and old problems. You must also demonstrate that the new techniques and approaches improve the performance of your department in one or more of the following ways:

A. Do the job faster,
B. Do the job easier,
C. Do the job more reliably,
D. Save money, or
E. Accomplish a new and highly desirable task (one that could not be done by the standard tools and techniques).

Remember to use techniques that will lend themselves to easy measurement. It is not sufficient to just bring about improvement. You must do it in a way that high-level management can understand and measure.

6. Absolute Personal Integrity

Your personal integrity must never be in question. Be completely honest in all of your business and personal dealings. If you ever have to choose between your loyalty to your immediate superiors and your personal integrity, always choose your personal integrity. When your superiors understand that your personal integrity is inviolable, they will place their trust in you. If you claim that you have brought about a significant improvement in your department, your superiors are much more apt to believe you if they have absolute confidence in your personal integrity.

Always remember that you are trying to demonstrate your fitness for a high-level management position. You must target the characteristics necessary for such a position and then demonstrate that you have them. The list of six characteristics given above is not exhaustive. You may have identified others that you think are necessary.

Add them to the above list. On a periodic basis, evaluate your own performance. Do you have each of the above characteristics? Are you adequately demonstrating them to your superiors? What are your plans both to acquire the characteristics and to demonstrate them? Look at high-level managers both in your own organization and in other organizations. Examine the characteristics that made them successful. Not all high-level managers demonstrate the same abilities, yet each was chosen to be advanced to high-level management. In most cases, the individual was advanced because the organization had a need, and high-level managers felt that the individual could satisfy that need. You are a unique individual, in the sense that no one else has the same background, training, and experiences that you do. Determine where your strengths lie. Focus your attention on a specific type of high-level management position that your background, training, and experiences would help you to achieve. Determine how you could best help the organization if you were a high-level manager.

Determine the kind of high-level position that your background, training, and experience would help you to gain. Examine whether you have the right qualifications and personal characteristics for that position. Work on acquiring the desired qualifications and personal characteristics.

You should plan out your route to success with at least the same vigour and determination that you use to set goals and determine plans for your own department. The management of your career is your personal responsibility, and you should invest both time and effort in it. Make a list of the characteristics that you wish to demonstrate to your superiors. Identify which ones you think that you have. Determine how to acquire those that you feel you do not currently have. Make plans to acquire the missing characteristics. Make specific plans that will demonstrate that you have the characteristics necessary for higher-level management. It is not just a matter of acquiring a list of accomplishments. You must demonstrate through your accomplishments that you have what it takes to be advanced to a high-level management position. Be prepared to use both the organizational and your private information system to help you accomplish your goals.

Work smart, not hard. Identify the characteristics that you need to demonstrate for a high-level management position. Plan how you will acquire these characteristics and how you will demonstrate them. Choose projects that will allow you to demonstrate these characteristics.

Since you are expected to be a traditional middle manager, anything that you do that is not traditional will draw attention to you. There are advantages and disadvantages to this. If you are successful and high-level management understands the reasons for your successes, you will be able to achieve your goals. If you are not successful, or if high-level management does not understand the reasons for your successes, then future attempts to be innovative and creative may be sharply curtailed. If you have squandered departmental resources in unsuccessful attempts to be innovative or creative, then you could be in deep trouble. It should be clear that you should carefully plan your nontraditional activities and should select only projects that exhibit a reasonable probability of success.

2.3 Conflict between the Traditional and the Nontraditional Roles

Even though most middle managers find themselves in a position where innovation and creativity are not expected of them, high-level management hopes that they will display these abilities. The middle manager therefore has two roles, and they are often in conflict with each other.

> The traditional role of getting the job done and the non-traditional role of exhibiting potential for a higher-level management position are often in conflict.

The traditional role of the middle manager is to direct the activities of a segment of the organization, but under the direction of a higher-level manager. The goals that the middle manager is expected to achieve are selected by or in conjunction with a manager at a higher level. The departmental plans to accomplish these goals are usually reviewed and approved by the higher-level manager. There is some latitude for creativity in the development of the departmental plans, but they still must be approved by the higher-level manager. The activities of the middle manager are supervised by, and therefore controlled by, the higher-level manager.

When someone must be selected to be advanced to a high-level management position, high-level management must either go outside the organization or must select a middle manager from within the organization. Even if they go outside the organization, it is still possible that they will choose a middle manager who has displayed the potential to handle a high-level management position. The middle manager must therefore perform the expected tasks in a satisfactory manner and still display the characteristics required for a higher-level management position. Unfortunately, performance of the expected tasks often requires that the middle manager "play it safe," leading not only to mediocre performance but also to a system that rewards the middle manager for exceptional mediocrity.

> Advancement based upon the attitude of "playing it safe" encourages mediocrity.

The individual advanced on the basis of following the rules must soon satisfy the Peter Principle, i.e., the individual must eventually be promoted to a position beyond his or her abilities. If you attempt to rise to the ranks of high-level management by playing it safe, i.e., by following the rules, you will not develop the characteristics necessary for advancement to high-level management, only to a dead-end position in middle management. You must take this problem into consideration before you develop your plans. The abilities that you need must be developed by finding and solving problems. Playing it safe and following the rules encourages you to avoid problems, thereby depriving you of the necessary educational opportunities and experiences.

Advancement based upon following the rules and playing it safe will eventually force you into a no-win situation. You will find yourself in a dead-end middle-management position where you do not have the abilities to handle the job.

Most of your contemporaries will seek to play it safe and will follow the rules. They may even seem to be promoted faster than you, but they will eventually satisfy the Peter Principle for the reasons stated above. One of your tasks will be to seek recognition and advancement outside of the ordinary (formal) route for advancement (the play-it-safe route). Why is it that so many innovative people find advancement by moving to another organization and then back to their original organization? Could it be that this is one of the informal promotion paths for the innovative?

Look for opportunities for advancement outside of the usual career path.

Be careful not to confuse company hopping, i.e., changing companies only for more money, with the principle being discussed here. The typical career path within an organization is one where you play it safe, do your job as expected, keep people happy, and eventually take your boss's place. What we are talking about here is a leap-frog effect, where you bypass your boss's position by moving to another organization with a position at your boss's level, and then moving back again at a higher level. I mention this kind of interorganizational mobility only because it emphasizes that nontraditional promotion paths are available to you. I do not advocate that you indiscriminately hop from one organization to another, but I do advocate that you form a plan that will allow you the flexibility of following either a traditional or a nontraditional career path.

> Do not indiscriminately hop from one company to another only in search of more money.

Luck is often a matter of seizing the opportunities. In many cases an innovative individual is recognized first by someone outside of his or her organization, and is offered a position in the other organization at a higher level and at a higher pay. In this situation you must weigh the potential of the opportunities in both organizations. The advantages of moving to another organization are clear: a higher position at a higher pay. The major disadvantage is that you might get the reputation of being a company hopper. If you move too often, others might feel that you will not stay with them long enough to be truly useful, and you will find your opportunities for further advancement limited. If you move from one company to another, do so as part of your plan for advancement, but also take advantage of unusual opportunities as they are presented.

CHAPTER 3

Standing out in the Organization

3.1 Adequate Performance of the Job Description

You must build a track record for reliability. This is usually accomplished by adequate performance of the assigned tasks. It is not necessary that you demonstrate a perfect record in all that you do, but it is necessary that you demonstrate that you can handle the fundamentals of your job. You must not fail in your basic, assigned tasks, for if you do, then your high-level management characteristics will be overlooked. In order to determine what your basic assigned tasks are, first determine how your job performance will be evaluated. Associated with each job, there are a small number of critical tasks. If these critical tasks are performed well, then you will receive a good evaluation. These critical tasks are chosen because they are important to the organization or for historical reasons. In addition, they are usually easy to measure. Determine the critical tasks, determine a reasonable level of performance, measure the level of performance constantly, and make sure that your performance is adequate.

You must not fail to perform your basic, assigned tasks in an adequate manner.

The reason that you must not be concerned about perfect performance is that such performance is just too difficult to be worthwhile. Let us assume that adequate performance accounts for n hours of effort on your part. In many occupations, perfect performance would then require at least 2n, or twice as many hours on your part. The trade-off here is that perfect performance, if it is possible at all, simply takes too much time. There is another good reason not to strive for perfect performance. There is an emotional drain associated with each level of performance. The harder that you strive for perfect performance, the larger the emotional drain. I suspect that the relationship between effort and emotional drain is not linear; doubling of the effort probably increases the emotional drain by a factor of four. Since most people run out of energy before they run out of time, it is important that you do not squander this important resource. It is hard to work intelligently if you are emotionally exhausted, and you must work intelligently to succeed.

> Aim for adequate performance of the basic tasks, rather than for perfect performance. Perfect performance, if it is even possible, simply takes too much of your time and energy.

Perfect performance might lead to promotion to another middle-level management position, but it seldom leads to promotion to high-level management positions. One reason that perfect performance does not lead to a high-level management position is the effect that the goal of perfect performance has on your department. Remember that you will need an increase in the number of workhours in order to increase the level of performance, so if you double the number of hours that your people have to work, then either you have to hire more people and the cost of operation goes up significantly, or personnel must work much longer hours. In the first case, you will get into trouble for spending too much money, since high-level management will not like a doubling of operational costs for a 10 percent increase in perform-ance. In the second case, you will lose experienced per-sonnel. The better certain people perform their jobs, the easier it will be for them to get jobs in other organiza-tions. If they suddenly have to work 80 hours a week, when they previously worked 40 hours a week, they will become unhappy and they will start looking for other jobs. This loss of trained personnel will bring about ex-actly the opposite of the desired effect, since the loss of key people will bring about a decrease in performance.

In any event, perfect performance seldom leads to pro-motion to high-level management. For example, an ac-countant might develop the skill necessary to account for every penny. The books always balance—there is never a missing penny. In this case, the accountant is usually re-warded with a pay raise, not a promotion. Accounting for every penny does not demonstrate either leadership potential or leadership skills. It does not demonstrate any of the characteristics necessary for a higher-level management position. In fact, it may actually demon-strate exactly the opposite.

> Perfect performance on the job seldom—if ever—leads to higher-level management positions.

3.2 Visibility

Visibility is the product of good performance. If you have visibility, then, when a task of a certain type needs to be performed, your superiors will think of you. The key here is to get a reputation for performance in areas that will either place you on the path to or lead directly to a high-level management position. A plan is very impor-tant if you wish to obtain a high-level management posi-tion. Evaluate each task and determine if it will help you get closer to your goals. The closer that good perform-ance will get you to your goals, the more time that you can afford to invest in the task. The degree of adequacy required by a task is related to how close your performance will get you to your goals. If performance of the task will not get you closer, then you should invest considerably less time in it than in a task that will directly get you into the desired management position. In any event, you must perform each assigned task, whether it is a part of your regular job or a special assignment, in an adequate manner.

The amount of time that you should invest in any specific assigned task must be determined by the final results. The amount of time that you invest should be related to the expected reward, which is movement toward a high-level management position.

You might find your career goals blocked by your own successes. You might find yourself trapped with a reputation for accomplishing a particular type of task, the accomplishment of which will not help you achieve your end goals. If you find yourself being assigned to accomplish these tasks on a regular basis, i.e., all of your time and efforts are going into these undesirable tasks and you do not have adequate time, energy or opportunity to achieve your own career goals, then you must take an appropriate action. You will need to state your hesitation to continue performing the undesirable tasks. If you continue to be assigned the undesirable tasks, then you will need to change departments, change jobs, or move to another organization.

If you are assigned tasks on a regular basis that keep you from accomplishing your career goals, then you will need to take an appropriate action. This may include moving to another organization.

3.3 Doing the Unusual

One way to achieve the desired kind of visibility is to gain a reputation for accomplishing the unusual. This may mean that you accomplish unusual tasks or that you employ unusual means to accomplish your tasks. The reputation for being able to do things differently must be coupled with the ability to do things in the conventional manner, when the situation calls for it. You do not wish to gain a reputation for being an oddball. You want to demonstrate flexibility and original thinking. You can gain the reputation for flexibility and original thinking without being considered as an oddball by performing ordinary tasks in the expected manner and by performing unusual tasks in an extraordinary manner. If you gain the reputation of being an oddball, then you will have difficulty advancing to a high-level management position, unless you can demonstrate that your techniques really work. As you move along the path toward a high-level management position, attempt to monitor the feelings that your superiors have concerning your performance. Attempt to have a balance between solid performance and creativity. If you have too much of one at the expense of the other, modify your plans in order to bring your performance in these two areas into balance.

Demonstrate the ability to perform ordinary tasks in the conventional manner and develop the reputation for being able to accomplish difficult tasks by the employment of unusual tools or techniques.

3.4 Doing Something that No One Else Can Satisfactorily Do

Many tasks are difficult because they are not thought about in the right way, rather than because they are inherently difficult. You want to understand the real nature of the problem, so that you can determine a real solution. If you attempt to solve a problem whose real nature you do not understand, then you will waste a considerable amount of time and energy. If you attempt to solve a problem before you understand its real nature, you may:

1. Not solve any problem at all,
2. Solve the wrong problem,
3. Solve only a portion of the problem, or
4. Take too much time, energy, and resources to solve the problem.

Problem solving consists of the following steps:

1.   Determine the Existence of a Problem

You certainly cannot solve a problem if you don't recognize that one exists. The recognition of the existence of a problem before it becomes too difficult to handle is one of the desired characteristics of a high-level manager.

2.   Determine the Nature of the Problem

Once you have determined the existence of a problem, examine the problem from a number of different viewpoints. Examine the symptoms of the problem first. From the symptoms determine the causes of the problem.

3.   Determine a Number of Solutions to the Problem

Once you understand the nature of a problem, you might then be able to determine a number of different solutions to the problem. It is not unusual to derive solutions that have trade-offs. One solution might require a large investment in resources, but allow a significant opportunity for success. Another solution might require a smaller investment in resources but allow a smaller opportunity for success. Some solutions might have an inverse relationship between time and money. If you invest a considerable amount of time in the project, then less money will be needed. Make a list of all of the solutions that you can think of.

4. Select a Solution that Has the Greatest Probability of Success

Because there will usually be a number of (possible) solutions for you to choose from, you will need to evaluate each solution on its relative merits. There will usually not be one best solution but several possible choices. Assign weights to each possible solution in order to determine the relative merits of each one. Then select a solution that can be implemented with the resources (time, energy, money, etc.) that you have.

5. Implement Your Solution

No solution is a good one unless it can and has been implemented. When I use the word *solution*, I am using it to mean a plan of attack to solve the problem. The plan, even if it is a good one, may or may not work, and its success cannot be determined until you have actually accomplished your plan. The implementation of a solution is putting your plan into action.

Problems might remain unsolved for any of the following reasons:

1. No One Recognizes that a Problem Exists

This is a good opportunity for you, since unrecognized problems are often easy to solve and their solution can make you look good. The suggestion box is an indication that there are always a number of unrecognized problems. Suggestions are usually important because they identify an area of need, rather than provide explicit solutions, so you should solicit suggestions for improvements from your workers.

2. The Problem Has Been Recognized, but No One Knows How to Solve It

This may be an area where a knowledge of information systems can be helpful. When you learn about information systems, you not only learn how they work, but you also gain an understanding of the kinds of problems that information systems can help solve. A problem might be unsolved because no one understands the nature of the problem clearly enough. A problem might also be un-solved because the technology has not advanced suffi-ciently for the implementation of a solution.

3. The Current Implementation of a Good Solution Is Faulty

It is not unusual to encounter situations where the prob-lem is well understood and the solution, at least on the logical level, is quite reasonable. Nevertheless, the solu-tion does not appear to work well. This is often because the implementation of the (logical) solution is not good. Let me give you an example from corporate information systems.

Problem.   Information systems constructed for man-agement take too long to build, cost too much, and are not specifically designed to help the manager do his or her task in the manner that the manager wants.

Solution.   Get the manager to participate in the con-struction of a new information system in a meaningful way.

Implementation of the Solution.   Have the manager read and sign each document produced during the analysis, design, and construction of the information system.

Both the identification of the problem and the solution to the problem are correct and reasonable, but there is a problem with the implementation. Most managers do not feel competent to read and critically evaluate the techni-cal documents associated with the construction of an in-formation system, so they just sign the documents with-out carefully reading them. Signing these documents without reading them does not lead to meaningful par-ticipation on the part of the manager. In fact, it may even cause trouble later on.

The technical people involved in the construction of the information system will probably feel that the signed document indicates that the appropriate people have approved the plans for the system. After the users become aware of problems with the system, they will inform the technical personnel. The technical personnel will then point to the documents, saying that they did exactly what was proposed in the documents. The technical people will feel justified by the documents, and the users will feel upset that they didn't get what they really wanted.

Learn to identify the critical stages of problem solving. Separate each of the following: the nature of the problem, the solution, and the implementation. Evaluate a solution and its implementation independently.

Doing something that no one else can do is often related to thinking about a problem in an unusual manner. Don't be bound by the conventional approach. This orients you toward a solution, when you must first understand the nature of the problem. You must understand the nature of the problem before you can create a solution of your own or understand someone else's solution. Also, never try to create or understand an implementation of a solution before you understand the solution itself. The first part of a task that you must come to grips with is understanding the nature of the problem to be solved.

Solutions to problems may happen by accident, but they usually happen because the problem solver has concentrated on the nature of the problem first, and then, having understood the problem, has derived a solution. Thinking about a problem in an unusual way means that you must not be guided by the traditional solutions, but rather by the nature of the problem itself. The following kinds of questions may be helpful in your attempts to understand the nature of a problem. Notice that these questions make no reference to a solution.

1. How was the problem discovered?
2. What are the symptoms of the problem?

3. With what organizational processes is this problem associated ?
4. Is this problem related to a problem that I have previously seen?
5. Do I recognize any of the subparts of the problem?

When attempting to solve a problem, ignore proposed and previous solutions (if there are any). Concentrate first on the nature of the problem, then derive a logical solution. Compare your solution with any solutions that may already be in existence. Rate your solution against the existing solutions and verify that yours is significantly better. Finally, concentrate on the implementation of your chosen solution.

The reason that you should examine the traditional solution (if there is one) after you have derived your own is that you might be too influenced by the traditional solution. I have found that if I examine the traditional solution before I derive my own solutions, then I am too prone to follow the path of the traditional solution. In such a case I have difficulty deriving any solutions that differ from the traditional one. If you have a solution that is different from and significantly better than the traditional one, then you have an accomplishment that will be recognized.

Compare your solution with the traditional one and see if your solution represents a significant improvement.

Be careful of management's approach to problem solving, since managers in positions higher than yours may be tied to traditional approaches. Each of the following stories illustrates this point:

1. Remember grandfather's old radio? It was so large that the cabinet for the radio was as large as an easy

chair. When radios where constructed in this manner, it was considered common knowledge that radios could never be made small enough to fit in automobiles. Eventually someone designed one that was small enough and made a considerable amount of money. Don't be limited by "common knowledge" or by traditional approaches.

2. Before World War II, an expert on rocketry was consulted by the British government as to whether there would be any threat of bombardment by rockets from the Continent. The "expert" was firmly of the opinion that it was impossible to build a rocket that could be used for that purpose. When the rockets first arrived, the British government asked for advice on how to counteract the problem. Guess who they asked? You guessed it—they sought advice from the "expert" who had informed them that such a rocket could never be built. Even in the face of gross incompetence, the traditional approach was to seek advice from the so-called expert.

3. There is a story that continues to circulate in engineering circles. For a number of years, a major manufacturer of light bulbs had been unable to frost the inside of a light bulb. Since so many people had unsuccessfully worked on the problem, it was considered to be an impossible task. As a joke, beginning engineers were assigned the task of frosting the inside of a light bulb. After a while, each new engineer gave up on the task and was then informed that the assignment was really a joke. Management felt that the experience was a good one, since it taught each new engineer humility and that some tasks were just too difficult to do. Eventually, a new engineer was hired, was assigned the task of frosting the inside of the light bulb, and successfully completed the task. The traditional assumption that the task could not be done was just plain wrong. It just hadn't been done yet.

In many cases, your attempts to be innovative and creative may not be met with favour, since your approach is not the traditional one. When you can show good, solid results, your approach will be looked at with much more favour.

3.5 Gaining a Reputation as a Doer

You must not only become visible in the organization, but you must do so in a manner that will enhance your position. You are a planner and an organizer. As such, you will need others actually to do much of the work that needs to be done. Cultivate a good relationship with those that you work with and with those that work for you. Reward good performance in a meaningful manner. Sometimes the reward will be a pay raise or a promotion, but most of the time the reward should be an honest expression of thanks for a job well done, public recognition of accomplishments, and/or notations in personnel files. Refrain from public criticism of those who work for you. It is much better to help them achieve their potential through suggestions and guidance for better performance. Work with your subordinates and help them set realistic goals for their own performance. Hold regular conferences with your subordinates so that they can evaluate their own progress. Encourage them to make plans to achieve their goals, and offer reasonable assistance when necessary. If you expect to be reasonably treated by your superiors, treat your subordinates in a similar manner. In terms of movement to higher management, this approach will build a firm foundation for your own progress. Use this approach to build personal loyalty between yourself and those that work for you. There is a strong relationship between the loyalty of those that work for you and your superiors' evaluation of your integrity. If you are trusted by your subordinates, then your superiors are more likely to trust you also.

> Build personal loyalty between yourself and those that work for you. It will become the foundation for your own success.

You must package your successes so that your superiors will become aware of them. This does not mean that you should broadcast your successes, but it does mean that you should make clear what your role was in each successful project in which you participated. When you complete a task, notify the appropriate people in writing that the task has been completed. State the nature of the project, problems encountered, problems solved, successes achieved, and your role in the project. Give credit by name to those who participated with you in the project, and send a copy of the report to appropriate subordinates. As you reward good work with recognition, your subordinates will feel more inclined to continue their good work. You must earn the trust, respect, and loyalty of your subordinates. Never make them feel that you are only using them in your climb to the top. If you help your subordinates in their climb to the top, they will be much more willing to help you. Remember that it is not necessary for you to accomplish something yourself (actually doing all of the work alone). It is probably enough to accomplish something good by carefully using the resources available to you. File a copy of each report as a part of your personal achievement file. You will need the reports in this file at a later time.

Report the completion of each task in writing. Give a copy of the report to those that helped in the project as well as to your superior. Include commendations in your reports for those that significantly contributed to the success of the project.

Create an achievement file. Keep a copy of all reports of successfully completed tasks in it.

All of your correspondence to your superiors concerning projects successfully completed should be designed to move you closer to your goal of a high-level management position. In your correspondence, emphasize those aspects of the project that demonstrate that you have the characteristics necessary for a high-level management position, but remember to do it with subtlety. You are not trying to broadcast your successes; you are only trying to highlight certain aspects of the project.

In your reports to your superiors, subtly highlight those parts of your reports that will indicate that you have the characteristics necessary for a high-level management position.

Before you write a project report or a proposal to your superiors, review your career plan. Determine which high-level management characteristics you wish to emphasize. If it is appropriate, phrase your report to emphasize the desired characteristics. Examine any parts of the project for failures. Do not be afraid of failures, as long as there have been significant successes also. It is fair to downplay your failures, as long as you don't try to make believe that they didn't happen. Be prepared to take the responsibility for your failures as well as for your successes. The ability to accept the consequences of your own actions is a large part of your personal integrity. Don't place the blame for a failure onto a subordinate, even if he or she really deserves it. Since you are the manager, you always have the ultimate responsibility for the success or the failure of a project. Let your superiors determine if the blame should be placed upon someone other than you.

Learn from your failures. Have a failure file as well as a success file and document your failures as carefully as you document your successes. Careful documentation of your failures will aid you in planning how to improve the performance of your subordinates and will serve as a reference that will help you avoid future failures. Each of us has our own strengths and weaknesses. Our failures help us to understand our weaknesses and will alert us to avoid certain difficulties. Advancement comes not only from successful achievements but also from the avoidance of areas in which we know we will not succeed. As you discover your own strengths and weaknesses, take advantage of your strengths, and strengthen or minimize your weaknesses. You can strengthen your weaknesses by gaining further education, training, and experience in the deficient areas, and you may minimize your weaknesses either by avoiding certain situations or by obtaining the help of knowledgeable personnel.

CHAPTER 4

A Primer on Information Systems

4.1 Definition of an Information System

Definition

An information system is a collection of people, procedures, instructions, and equipment that will produce information in a useful form.

People are considered to be part of an information system because it takes people to make an information system work. People gather the raw data, enter the data into
the system, and either process the data or make sure that
it is processed correctly. The design of an information
system must be people-oriented. Every facet of the system must be easy to use, and the instructions must be
clear.

The entry of data into an information system is often considered to be a minor part of the total operation. This is
unfortunate, since a poor quality of data leads to a poor
quality of reports (information). A descriptive phrase for
this situation is "garbage in, garbage out."

In every information system, there is a collection of
procedures. These procedures actually process and report
the data, or they specify just how the data is to be processed and reported. In an information system that uses a
computer, the procedures often appear as programs.

Instructions are the directions for use of the system.
The instructions specify:

1. The form of the input data,
2. The order in which procedures are to be performed,
3. The times and dates that the procedures are to be performed,
4. The distribution of reports,
5. Special handling procedures, and
6. How to recover in case of a system error.

The *equipment* used in an information system may include anything from special pens and forms for the recording of the data to special devices, such as calculators and computers, for the processing of the data. Not all information systems utilize computers, so we may distinguish between two different kinds of information systems.

Definition
We will call an information system a *manual system* if it does not use a computer to perform any of the procedures, and we will call an information system an *automated system* if a computer is used to perform at least one of the procedures.

It is difficult to imagine an information system of any size that does not use a computer to perform at least one of the procedures. This is because of the speed and reliability of computerized processing. Essentially all automated systems have a number of procedures that are performed manually, since human intervention is a necessary ingredient of any information system. Humans have the ability to apply subjective tests and to make subjective decisions, but computers do not have this ability. In any information system, a number of situations might arise that require subjective actions. This is one major reason that the use of machines must be balanced with the use of people. Information systems which are too heavily computerized are often so inflexible as to be difficult to use. In modern information systems, there will be a variety of equipment, including: forms for the gathering of data, pens and pencils, typewriters, filing cabinets, data entry devices, printers, and computers.

Data must be converted into a useful form in order for it to be information. Most of the time data must be processed in order for it to become useful. For example, consider retail sales.

A chain of stores sells retail products on a nationwide basis. In each store, sales are recorded at the cash registers. When a sale is made (or when an item is returned), the department code and the item identification is entered. The item cost is obtained either from a file in the cash register (if a sale) or from the sales receipt (if a return). A number of people in the organization need to receive information derived from the retail sales.

1. Inventory control receives a computerized file that is used to update inventory amounts. The records in this file consist of the store number, the department number, individual inventory item numbers, and the quantity of each item sold. This file is in a form that can be read directly by a computer and is used to keep track of the quantity of each item on hand at each store.

2. Each store department receives a periodic listing of items sold. This report includes the beginning and ending dates of the sale period, the identification number, description, quantity, sale price and profit of each item sold, and a total departmental profit figure.

3. Each store manager receives a periodic report that shows the beginning and ending dates for the sales period and the sales figures for each department, including the department number and profit figure. The individual item amounts are not included in this report.

4. Each regional manager receives a periodic report that shows the sales figures for each store in the region. This report includes the beginning and ending dates of the sales period and the sales figures for each store, including the store number and profit figure. The individual department amounts are not included in this report.

5.   The president of the organization receives a periodic
     report that shows the sales figures for each region. This
     report does not include individual store information.

The reports are tailored to the individual needs of the recipients. The original (raw) sales data may be sorted, used
in arithmetic operations, arranged in a file, included in a
report, summarized, or filtered in order to produce the required information.

Definition
Information is considered to be *useful* if it satisfies all of the
following:

1.   It is wanted by the recipient,
2.   It is needed by the recipient,
3.   The recipient knows how to use it,
4.   It is in the form desired by the recipient,
5.   It is sufficiently timely, and
6.   It is accurate.

If data is not useful, then it will probably be ignored.
We will see later that lack of usefulness of the information provided by the organization's information system
is one of the reasons for the construction of your own
private information system.

In some cases, the technical personnel involved in the construction of an information system may feel that they know
more about what the information system should do than the
people for whom the system is being built. This is a totally
absurd assumption. I know of a case where a department
within a large military base needed to have an information
system built for them. The analysis and design was done by
one person, and this person had the attitude that he knew
in advance just what the department needed. He refused to
listen to the members of the department, since he felt that
he knew more than they did. He was going to build a system that he knew they needed, not the one that they said
they needed. After the system was completed, not one
member of the department ever used it. They refused to use
it because they did not perceive it as being helpful to them.
Because the members of the department were not allowed to

participate in the design of the information system, they
didn't want it.

4.2 Software

Definition
The programs used in an information system are called *software*. Software is divided into two main categories: *application* software and *system* software.

Application software is a collection of programs that
have been written especially to meet your specific information needs. System software is the collection of programs that allows the programmers to write an application system for you. System software includes the following: (1) the operating system, (2) a programming language, and (3) a facility for handling files of data.

Definition
An *operating system* is a program in the computer that asks you the question, "What do you wish to do next?" It takes your response to the question and attempts to satisfy your request. All of the facilities of the computer are available through the operating system. Without the operating system, the computer is just an unusable collection of electronic circuits.

Definition
The *programming language* software allows the programmer to write programs for you. This software takes a program and converts it into a set of instructions that the computer can deal with directly.

Definition
A computer is said to *execute* or run a program when it carries out the instructions contained in the program.

A facility for handling files of data is always provided
by the manufacturer of your computer. It is invoked by
the operating system whenever you wish to access files
of data stored within the computing system. In addition

to the data handling facility provided by the manufacturer of your computer, specialized *database management* or *file management* systems may be used in your computer. The database and file management systems are designed to help the programmer organize and access data. The purpose of such systems is to allow you to store data in a manner that will:

1. Ensure fast access to the data,
2. Minimize problems with adding, deleting, and changing the data, and
3. Allow you to access the data in unanticipated ways.

Database and file management systems are very popular on both large and small computers. Further discussions on the use of database and file management systems will appear in Chapters 7 and 8.

4.3 Hardware

Definition
A *computer system* consists of a computer, its system software, and all of the devices attached to the computer that allow you to enter, store, and display data.

Definition
Computer *hardware* is the collection of physical (nonsoftware) components of the computer system.

Computer hardware is divided into three main categories:

1. The computer itself,
2. Devices for communicating with the computer (called I/O or Input/Output devices), and
3. Storage.

Each of these three categories of hardware will appear in every information system.

The computer, no matter what its size, will have different kinds of specialized circuitry, including a central processor and main memory. The *central processor* is the circuitry that executes your programs. *Main memory* is the area within the computer itself where programs and their associated data are stored while the programs are being executed.

Communication (or *I/O*) devices allow you to enter data and instructions into the computer and to display the results of your instructions. Common types of communication devices are the *terminal* and the *printer*. A terminal is a device with a keyboard and a method of displaying the communication to and from the computer. The terminal may have a televisionlike screen for the display (called a CRT) or it may print in a manner similar to a typewriter. A printer is a device that allows you to produce a printed copy of the communication from the computer. Printers are often used in conjunction with CRT terminals, allowing a permanent copy of the communication from the computer (usually the reports). Since the typewriterlike terminal is usually too slow to print large reports, printers are often used with this type of terminal, too.

A (secondary) storage device allows you to store both large and small data files over a period of time. Such devices are designed to store the data after you have shut off the computer, so that it will be available at a later date. Typical kinds of storage devices are *disk* and *tape*. Disk allows fast access to data at a moderate price, and tape allows slow access to data at a low price. The cost of disk units on both large and small computers has come down so much in recent years that virtually all business computers use them for the storage of data. Tape is commonly used now for historical files or for a backup copy of critical information. It is seldom used for the storage of information that must be accessed on a regular basis. The reason for the speed advantage of disk over tape is that data can be accessed either sequentially or directly on disk but only sequentially on tape.

Access is said to be *direct* if the address or location of the data on the disk can be used to access the data. If access is direct, the computer either computes the address of the data or looks up the address in a table. The address is then given to the disk unit, and the disk unit returns the data to the computer. The information on a disk is arranged in the form of concentric circles. A device called a head is moved to the position (circle) where the data is stored. The disk itself is rapidly rotated about its center. When the head is located over the proper circle (actually called a track) and the disk has rotated to the correct position, then the data is transferred from the disk to the computer. Transfer of data from the computer to the disk is accomplished in a similar manner. Access is said to be *sequential* if, in order to access a particular record, you must access all of the records that precede it. When you access data stored on a magnetic tape, you first look at record number one. If this is not the data that you want, then you look at each succeeding record, one at a time, until you either find the record that you want or until you determine that the data is not on the tape.

The processing of data is often classified by the type of access used. Thus, processing may be called direct or sequential. Both types of processing are in common use today, since some applications are fast and inexpensive if sequential access is used and other kinds are fast and inexpensive if direct access is used. The kind of processing that you will do on your own private information system will be determined by your applications, but I expect that most of it will be direct rather than sequential.

4.4 Types of Problems Solved by Information Systems

There are a number of different kinds of problems that people solve through the use of information systems (actually, the computer is used to implement the solutions). They include, but are not limited to:

1. The processing and storage of daily transactions (daily paper handling),
2. The production of reports to management,

3. The retrieval of information,
4. Complex or tedious mathematical operations,
5. The sorting or arranging of large volumes of data, and
6. The support of decision making.

The first general application of computers in the business environment was automation of the accounting function and its related processes, including the handling of the organization's financial transactions. The reasons that this function was automated first are:

1. The procedures and algorithms used in accounting were both definitive and well understood, and
2. A large number of workhours could be saved if the procedures were to be automated (there was a reasonable expectation that the return would exceed the investment).

This first attempt at automation was then broadened to include the organization's daily transactions. A common example is the inclusion of sales and inventory:

Each time an item is sold, a record of the sale is made and entered into the information system. The sales information is used to update the inventory quantities, to record the sales information itself, and to update the appropriate journals and ledgers. In many organizations, this is thought of as a direct extension of the accounting function itself.

As the volume of the daily transactions grew, it became clear that the raw material for managerial reports was already being stored by the computer system. The *transaction processing systems*, i.e., the information systems whose main purpose was the processing of the daily transactions, were then modified to produce reports designed specifically for supervisors and middle management. This was accomplished through the addition of (application) programs that were designed to utilize the data gathered from the processing of the daily transactions and transform this data into a form useful to low and middle levels of management. When a transaction processing system has been modified to produce reports designed specifically for management, it is usually called a *management information system (MIS)*.

No matter how carefully an information system is designed, there will always be some information needs not specifically addressed and met by the system. One of the advantages of a modern information system is a facility for the nonprogrammer to directly access the data files to obtain answers to the unanticipated data needs. The facility for accomplishing access to a computerized data file by nonprogrammers is called a *query system*. Query systems, depending upon the type, allow the nonprogrammer to access data in a variety of ways and to print out simple reports automatically. The nonprogrammer describes the data that is wanted, and the query system obtains the desired data and formats it into a readable report. Some training is required to make effective use of a query system, but specific training in programming is not required. A query facility is clearly an important part of a private information system.

Since the management information system is based upon the data gathered from the processing of daily transactions, there are problems faced by both middle- and high-level management that cannot be directly aided by such a system. These problems often require information that is not gathered by the management information system, either because the system was not designed to gather it or because the information simply is not available within the organization. In the first case, a modification of the current information system might make the necessary information available. In the second case, no modification of the current information system will make the information available. Research is underway to develop information systems that primarily use information not available within the organization itself, but there does not yet appear to be any large working systems of this type commonly in use.

In general, information systems can be used to assist

in the decision-making function by: (1) providing the requisite information, (2) simulating activities, (3) forecasting, (4) trend analysis, (5) etc.

4.5 Types of Computers

There is no good criteria or definition that distinguishes between large and small computers, so most people use cost for this purpose. Large computers often cost £500,000 or more, mid-sized computers cost approximately £100,000 to £500,000, minicomputers cost approximately £10,000 to £100,000, and microcomputers usually cost up to £10,000. Personal microcomputers may cost under £50, and microcomputers suitable for the business environment usually cost £1,000 or more. Any technique used to distinguish between different types of computers has trouble with areas of overlap. For example, there may be an inexpensive minicomputer that costs less than an expensive microcomputer. Computers that cost £15,000 or more often have one basic type of construction, while microcomputers have a different type of construction. The microcomputer derives its name from the type of processor (the part that executes programs) used in it. The entire processor is contained on one integrated (micro) circuit. Using the type of processor to distinguish between certain types of computers will probably not be possible within a few years. Since it is cost effective to put the entire processor on one integrated circuit, and since the technology necessary to place complex processors on an integrated circuit is advancing rapidly, all computers will eventually have their processor on one integrated circuit.

Advances in technology have made it possible to produce small, low-cost computers that are more powerful than a number of the more expensive computers that were produced just a few years ago. Most organizational information systems use large or mid-sized computers because they deal with large volumes of data. Since the large computers are faster than the small computers, the large volume of data and the processing time requirements have precluded the use of the small (micro) computers as part of the organization's information system. Since you will be using a microcomputer for your private information system, it is appropriate to discuss this type of computer in greater depth.

Microcomputer software and hardware have made rapid advances since the late 1970s. A comparison of the early microcomputers (circa 1970) with current microcomputers is given in the following table, where K is approximately 1,000 and M is approximately 1 million. Measurements for disk space and main memory are given in bytes, which corresponds to characters of storage.

	Early Micros	Current Micros
Cost	About £10,000	£400 to £1,500
Disk space	70K	Up to 50M
Main memory	8K	Up to 900K
Relative speed	Slow	Fast

There are currently three major types of microcomputers, the 8-bit machine, the 16-bit machine, and the 32-bit machine. The number of bits indicates the size of the data and instructions that may be moved within and executed by the computer. Of the three machines, the 32-bit microcomputer is noticeably faster than the 16-bit microcomputer and the 16-bit microcomputer is noticeably faster than the 8-bit microcomputer. The IBM AT is an example of the new 32-bit microcomputers. Several of the most popular mid-sized computers today are 32-bit machines. The modern microcomputer (compared with the earlier microcomputer) is relatively fast, as a result of each of the following: faster processor, faster transfer rate for data, more main memory, and faster disk access.

There are two types of disk storage commonly in use today: floppy disk and hard disk. Many microcomputers use floppy disks as their only type of secondary storage, mainly because of the cost. A microcomputer with one floppy disk and one hard disk may cost from £600 to £1,200 more than one with two floppy disks. Computers other than the microcomputer always use hard disks for secondary storage because hard disks hold much more data and are much faster than floppy disks. The hard disks on larger computers may hold as much as 250M bytes of information. The hard disk on a microcomputer usually holds 5M to 15M bytes, but 50M-byte units do exist. Advances in disk technology will soon allow low-cost, high-capacity replacements for both floppy and hard disks.

Since microcomputers cost so much less than the larger computers, it is possible for a greater number of people to purchase one. A small company can develop system software for a microcomputer with a very small investment. This means that the number of software packages that you might use to build your own private information system is considerably greater with a micro-computer than with any other kind of computer. The variety and availability of software for the microcomputers has both advantages and disadvantages. The major disadvantage is that the beginner has no way to determine which software is good and which is bad. I consider software to be good if it: (1) has low cost, (2) works correctly, (3) is easy to use, (4) is powerful (performs a number of different functions), and (5) is fast.

The major advantage of the variety of available software is that it is possible to obtain software with each of these five characteristics. When you purchase comparable software for a large computer, the cost for the software may be from 10 to 5,000 times more expensive than (reasonable) comparable software on a microcomputer, and software for the microcomputer is invariably easier to use. The larger computers with their expensive software are usually faster when large volumes of data are involved, but, since we expect to have relatively small amounts of data in private information systems on microcomputers, this is usually not an important factor.

Hardware Selection

My personal opinion is that essentially all private information systems can be built using appropriate software and a single microcomputer system with the following characteristics:

1. Main memory at least 256K (but 512K is recommended),
2. A 16-bit processor (32-bit, when good software is available),
3. One floppy and one hard disk drive,
4. A modem, and
5. A printer.

A modem is a device that allows you to communicate with the computer used by your organization, assuming that the information system developed by your organization is modern enough to allow access to the computer and the stored data through such a device. With special communications software and a modem, you can communicate with your organization's computer as if your microcomputer were an ordinary terminal. You will also be able to transfer data between the organization's computer and your own computer with this facility. The use of the modem will be further explained in Chapter 7.

If you purchase an IBM XT or compatible computer, it appears that you will have no difficulty obtaining appropriate system development software. You may choose one kind of computer over another kind for a number of reasons, including price and additional features.

I would usually hesitate to recommend a specific kind of computer to a wide audience, but it is clear that most developers of new software are targeting their software to the IBM (PC or XT) compatible microcomputers. The good software that has been around for a few years is also available for the IBM compatible computers, so the choice of an IBM or compatible microcomputer will probably ensure that the desired software development system will be available. You must be careful when purchasing an IBM compatible computer. A number of computer manufacturers claim that their product is IBM compatible. Some of these microcomputers really are compatible, and some are not. I had an experience where a salesman from a reputable manufacturer of microcomputers claimed that his machine was "nearly 100 percent IBM compatible." The claim was that almost all of the programs that run on the IBM PC would run on his machine. I tried five standard software packages on his machine, and not one of them worked. I only know one way to determine if a microcomputer is IBM compatible: this is on an application-by-application basis. Obtain a copy of the system development software and see if it will run on your choice of computer. Perform this test before you make any agreements to purchase a microcomputer, not after.

4.6 Database and File Management Systems

There are two major problems associated with the computerized storage of data: access to the data must be fast, and data items that are logically related must be stored in a manner that reflects this logical relationship. One aspect of speed of access to data is the duplication or redundancy of the data. If data is often duplicated within the system, then certain types of access are fast, but then there is a potential problem with having copies of certain data items. If the data is duplicated, then changing a data item may require that the same change be made in a number of places, increasing the time required for effecting the changes. If the changes are not properly made to each copy of the data, then the copies of the data may, at times, not all agree with each other. The logical relationship must either be explicit in the storage structure or it must be possible to recreate the logical relationship as needed. Database and file management systems are specialized system software that help you solve these two problems. The primary emphasis of this type of system software is to create the relationships between data items so that a number of different relationships can be preserved. Most database and file management systems are still relatively slow, but the power provided from the association of related but different data items makes the speed of the systems tolerable.

The operating systems for your microcomputer and for your organization's computer allow you to access standard data and program files. The access to the files is provided through special system utilities. When you request through the operating system, for example, that the contents of a file be displayed on the screen of your terminal, the operating system calls (executes) a system utility to perform this function for you. This facility is easy to use since it uses, in a transparent manner, primitive functions for accessing data and program files. These same primitive functions are available to the creators of database and file management systems, allowing them to store and access data independently of the operating system and in a variety of ways. The three most common types of database management systems are relational, hierarchical, and network systems. The most common file management system is the indexed file system.

Your software technician will select either a database or a file management system for your microcomputer. The selection will probably be based upon your specific needs, the type of microcomputer that you will use, and the past experiences of the software technician. The criteria for the selection of the database or file management system should include each of the following:

1. A controlled duplication or redundancy of the data should be allowed. The system should allow the technician to decide if certain data items will be duplicated in order to increase the speed of certain critical operations.

2. It should be possible to fine tune the system to make it efficient for you and your workers to use.

3. If something goes wrong with your information system (this will eventually be the case), there should be utilities associated with your system to help you rebuild your data files. If your system should fail, it should fail gracefully, i.e., it should notify you that there is a problem and help you to recover from the problem.

4. The system should contain the features that you want, such as a graphics or a spreadsheet capability, or it

should be able to interface or communicate with a standard package that provides the desired capability. You and the software technician must decide together what features you want to have in your private information system.

5. Your system should have a good query capability associated with it. No matter how carefully you and the software technician plan your private information system, there will always be some data needs not directly addressed by your system. A good query capability will allow you to access the needed data on an ad hoc basis.

6. Your system should contain special utilities that will allow your technician to easily restructure the data files. Your understanding and the understanding of your technician will evolve over a period of time. As both of you come to understand your information needs better, some restructuring of the data will be necessary. Special utilities that aid in this restructuring are very helpful.

The Relational Database Management System

The relational database management system stores the data in flat files. A flat file is a file that stores data in the form of a table. Each line or row of the table represents one record. Each record consists of a collection of fields, and the number and the order of the fields in each record in one file match the number and the order of the fields in any other record in that file. The fields of a record contain the individual data items, such as social security number, name, and address. A column in a flat file consists of all the fields of a certain type. For example, if we have a file with records that have the social security number in the first field, then the first column of the flat file consists of all of the social security numbers of all the employees in our file. In addition, the intersection of a row with a column yields a specific data item value; the intersection of the first row with the first column in our current example would yield the social security number in the first record. Special operators are provided that allow us to associate records in one file (actually called a relation in the terminology of the relational

database system) with records in another file and to select specific rows (records) and columns (fields) from
existing files.

The relational database system has, in the past, been
too slow to be useful with large volumes of data, but advances in speed techniques will soon make fast relational
database management systems available. With relational
database systems it is easy to add new records, modify
existing records, delete records, and restructure files.

The Hierarchical Database Management System

The hierarchical database management system was the
first commercially available database system. Data is arranged in a fixed, treelike fashion, preserving the
hierarchical relationship between data items. This system
has no distinct files, except for the entire database. The
data items (fields) are arranged into records in the normal
manner, like a single row of a relational database file, and
the records are physically arranged in a contiguous manner. Assume that we have three types of data in our database: employee information, information about the children of each employee, and information concerning the
skills of each employee. One possible hierarchical database structure for this type of data is to store the data for
the first employee first, followed immediately by the information for the children of this employee (one record
for each child), followed immediately by the skill information for this employee (one record for each skill), and
then to store the data for all of the remaining employees in
a like manner, with all of the employee, child, and skill
information for each employee grouped together.

The hierarchical database system is quite fast for certain types of access (like finding the skills that a certain
employee has), but it can be extremely slow for other
types of access (like finding the names of all employees
that have a certain skill). Because hierarchical database
systems have a fixed and contiguous arrangement of data
records, adding new records and deleting records can be
a time-consuming process. When records are added to an
existing database, they are placed in a special temporary

area, to be inserted into the actual database at a later time. Restructuring the database is always time consuming and, in some cases, is rather difficult. Modification of the contents of a record in the database is easily and quickly accomplished.

The Network Database Management System

The network database management system has different types of records but only one file, the database file. Records that are logically related to each other in the mind of the user are often physically related within the database file. Related data records are arranged in sets. For example, one set might have one employee record as the owner and several skill records as the members. The database management system helps you to find the employee record that you are interested in, and then it helps you to find the members, one at a time, of the set that contains that employee record and the associated skill records. The employee, the child, and the skill records can reside anywhere on the disk or in main memory of the computer. The relationship between an owner and the members of a set is preserved by a pointer (linkage) from the owner to the first member of the set, then from each member of the set to the next member, and finally from the last member back to the owner (in a circular fashion). Since relationships are determined by the sets and since the relationships are implemented in the form of pointers, a single record can be an owner of several different kinds of sets and a member of several different kinds of sets. Extremely complex relationships can then be implemented within a network database system, and it is easy to add records, delete records, and modify the contents of records. In many cases, it is easy to restructure the database file. Access to records in the database is quite fast. The major disadvantage of this type of database system is its frightening complexity. As the number of different types of records and as the number of relationships grows, the structure of the database becomes harder and harder for the nonprogrammer to understand. Many types of query systems for the network database management system require the user to understand all of the relationships between different types of records. If the complexity is sufficiently great, this may make it difficult for you to use such a query system.

File Management Systems

The most popular kind of file management system is the indexed file system. The data is stored in flat files, logically in the same form as that used in the relational database management system. The associations between related records of different types is obtained through the use of the index files. An index file is a special auxiliary (nondata) file that is used to facilitate access. Assume that we have three files: an employee file, a child file, and a skill file. The social security number of a specific employee will appear in the record for this employee in the employee file, in the record for each child of this employee in the child file, and in the record for each skill of this employee in the skill file. An index for the child file and an index for the skill file make it possible to quickly find the child and the skill information associated with a specific employee. Whenever you wish to preserve a particular relationship between different types of records, use an existing index or create a new one.

In this type of system, it is easy to add a new record, delete a record, modify a record, and restructure a file. Access to related records is quite fast. In the past, the major drawback for this kind of system has been the extra disk space required by the index files (they can be quite large) and the time required to add a record to or delete a record from an indexed file. The problems of extra disk space and slow deletion of records still exist, but recent advances have caused new indexed file systems to appear on the market that are extremely fast for the addition of new records to files.

Remarks on Database and File Management Systems

No database or file management system can be all things to all people. A system that is right for someone else might not be right for you. In addition, the choice of a database or file management system will depend upon your own specific data needs. I recommend that you and your technician analyze your data needs first, and then have the technician select a good database or file management system to meet your specific needs. Do not purchase a database or file management system before you select a software technician, since you may then need to purchase another system later, after the analysis of your data needs has been completed. For a more complete discussion of database and file management systems, refer to the book, *Database and File Management Systems*, by Nelson T. Dinerstein, Scott, Foresman, 1984.

CHAPTER 5

A Primer on the Technical Abilities of the Software Technician

5.1 Introduction

It is appropriate for you to be familiar with two of the major tasks of the software technician, analysis and design, and you should be acquainted, to some degree, with the concepts of programming and testing. You certainly don't have to be an expert in each of these areas, but it will be helpful to have a knowledge of analysis, design, programming, and testing when you interview candidates for the position of software technician and during the entire process of constructing the private information system. This chapter is designed to introduce you to the nature of the problems to be solved, to the terminology, and to the modern techniques for solving the problems. By the time that you have read this chapter you should have gained enough knowledge about these topics to feel comfortable when interviewing a candidate or when discussing problems with the software technician.

You don't have to be an expert in analysis, design, and programming, but, if you know something about each of these areas, then you will be better able to select a good software technician and you will facilitate communication between yourself and the technician.

5.2 Analysis

The purpose of analysis is to determine the condition of your current information system, your information needs, and how the current information system falls short of your information needs. The software technician will probably start the process of gathering facts about the current information system by having an interview with you. It is therefore appropriate for you to be familiar with the rudiments of the organization's information system. You must have enough knowledge to at least start the software technician in the right direction. Gather together as much technical and user documentation for the organization's information system as you can. The more information that you can gather in written form, the less that you will personally need to know. Also include a copy of each report that you receive from the organization's information system and be prepared to discuss its purpose, how you use it, and your evaluation of it.

Before the software technician arrives, gather as much written information as you can concerning the organization's information system.

The software technician will organize, read, analyze, and evaluate all of the material that you can provide, but he or she will also need to speak to the personnel in your department who are familiar with the organization's information system. If I were your software technician, I would want to talk directly to you to get your personal picture of the organization's information system, then I would like to talk to a number of individuals in your department to get similar information. In many cases, it is best for the software technician to interview you first, then some of the people that report directly to you, then some of the people that report directly to those that report to you, and so on. When an individual knows that the software technician has the permission of his or her direct superior for the interview, then the individual is usually cooperative. At first glance it would appear that each individual in your department would cooperate with the software technician just because the software technician is working on a project for you, but that is seldom the case. You and the software technician will need to create the right atmosphere for individual cooperation, but the creation of the right atmosphere will be mainly your responsibility. It may also be necessary for the software technician to talk to the organization's software development people, but you may find that you have little or no influence with them. Their reaction to discussing the organization's information system with your software technician might range from complete cooperation to outright hostility; but, in the majority of cases, their reaction will range from a lack of time for the discussions to outright hostility. The majority of help for the software technician will therefore come from you and your department.

> The creation of an atmosphere in which the members of your department and the software technician will work together cooperatively is mainly your responsibility.

Explain to the members of your department what your general plans are for the improvement of working conditions within the department. Assure them that the purpose of the forthcoming changes will be to make individual work assignments easier. If some of your subordinates are concerned that their jobs might be eliminated, be willing to discuss their concerns with them in private. Such concerns are real to some of your subordinates and should be handled with respect and courtesy. Assure your managers that their jobs cannot be eliminated by computers and that they will have a new opportunity both to learn about computers and to develop their own creative abilities. Remember that helping others to get ahead should be as much a part of your plans as is helping yourself to get ahead. The workers that are neither in managerial nor supervisory positions in your department may also fear that their jobs might be eliminated. It may be appropriate for their individual supervisors to talk to those concerned on an individual basis, assuring them that every effort will be made to reassign them within the department or organization, rather than let them go, if their job is eliminated. The fear of losing one's job is real and will not go away. You must be prepared to handle it in a reasonable and rational manner, taking the feelings of the concerned individuals into consideration. Learn as much as you can about the kinds of jobs that might be eliminated (if any), and make advance preparations to help the individuals concerned. Don't put this off until the last minute, but include it in your master plan for the departmental reorganization.

If it appears that some of the members of your department will lose their current jobs due to your new private information system, make plans early to help the individuals concerned.

During the interview processes, the software technician will ask selected members of your department what they do and how they do it. The questions may vary with each individual being interviewed, but the basic information being sought is the same:

1. What information is needed to do the job?
2. Where does the information come from?
3. What form is the information in?
4. Is the information clear, concise, on time, easy to get, etc.?
5. Specifically how is the information used?
6. Is any processing or manipulation of the data necessary, or is it already provided in the proper form?
7. Is there any missing data, i.e., does the individual need data which is not available?
8. If more data is needed, where can it be obtained and what form should it be in?

9.   Does the information produced or used by the individual get passed on to anyone else?

If you know in advance the kinds of questions that the software technician will ask, then you can be prepared to answer some of them yourself. You will be able to answer the questions as they pertain to your own job, but you should let others answer for themselves. There is always a gap between a manager's perspective of a job and the perspective of the individual who performs it, because of the differences between the concept and the implementation of the job. Be prepared for conflicting opinions on jobs. You, as the manager of the department, may have one viewpoint of what a worker does, the supervisor of the worker may have a second viewpoint, and the worker may have a third. Don't be upset or offended if this occurs. A number of viewpoints of a job are to be expected and may be beneficial, since everyone concerned can gain a greater understanding of the function of the task.

Expect that there will be differences between a manager's perception of a job and the perception of the individual doing the job.

Prepare in advance for the interviews. Provide a neutral place for most of the interviews, but don't insist that all of the interviews be performed there. Most of the people in the department will wish to have short interviews during working hours but, in some cases, it might be better for an interview to be performed in another location or at a time other than during normal working hours. The location for the interviews should be quiet, and the interviews should take place without interruption. Telephone calls should be routed to the individual being interviewed only in case of real emergency. Inform the individuals in advance of the types of questions that they will be asked, so that they can prepare for the interview. Provide help to those who will be interviewed so that they will understand what is expected of them. It is not sufficient for them to be commanded to be helpful to the software technician. You must help them to get organized by providing them with reasonable guidelines and by providing a way for them to get their questions answered, but make it clear that you expect everyone to cooperate.

You can help the software technician in the interview process if you can describe the goals and plans of your department. You will understand much more about your department than will the software technician. Help the technician to understand your department as a system and as a subsystem of the organization. Provide a hierarchical diagram of the management structure of your department to the technician. Include names of individuals, titles, job descriptions, and the reporting structure. The hierarchical diagram will be used by the software technician in planning an interview schedule. Once the schedule has been planned, you, as the manager of the department, will need to inform the individuals concerned and will need to make preparations for the interviews. Make sure that the individuals are prepared for the interviews, that a satisfactory place has been provided for the interviews (if necessary), and that sufficient time has been provided for the interviews.

Providing time for the interviews will be one of the hardest parts of the preparation. Most people will feel that they just don't have time for the interview. The longer that the interview goes, the more uncomfortable they will feel. Once, when I was interviewing someone, the individual jumped up after 10 minutes and ran out of the room, mumbling something about how he didn't have time for this foolishness and just had to get back to the job. In some cases, it will be necessary for a manager or supervisor to provide extra help to individuals so that their workload will be temporarily reduced. This will, in many situations, reduce the fear that work is piling up and that they just don't have time for the interview. It will be your responsibility to arrange for the extra resources in advance.

> Provide extra help to the members of your department so
> that they feel that they have the time to be interviewed by
> the software technician.

One of the tasks of the software technician is to create an
information flow diagram for your department. The purpose of this diagram is to record the movement of data and
information into, within, and out of your department. In
its original form, the diagram may contain the names of
documents and the names of individuals or subdepartments. This diagram will then be refined until all of the
data is represented by an abstract description and the
names of individuals and subdepartments are replaced by
descriptions of the functions that they perform.

Assume, as an example, that you are the manager of a
credit department for a bank. During an interview with a
worker named Mary, the software technician discovers
that Mary receives an exception report, called the *credit
exception report*, from John. The exception report contains a list of accounts that have charges over the credit
limit, and Mary has the responsibility to determine what
action to take. For an individual account, she might:

1. Increase the credit limit and inform the account
   holder of the action,
2. Keep the credit limit where it is and inform the
   account holder that the account has charges in excess of the credit limit, or
3. Freeze the account and inform the account holder
   that no further charges will be accepted until the
   credit balance has been reduced below a specified
   level.

The part of the information flow diagram that represents
this situation is given by Diagram 5.1.

John gets the report from the computer and verifies
that Mary has not taken an action for the accounts on the
report within the last three days. If an action has been

DIAGRAM 5.1

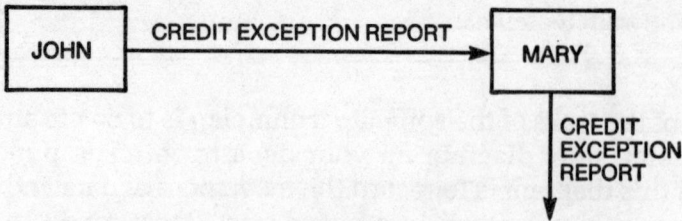

taken for an account within the last three days, the account number has a line drawn through it. When Mary gets the report, she examines each account that does not have a line drawn through it and makes a notation on the report as to the action to be taken. Copies of the report are made and routed to the appropriate individuals. The final diagram might now have the form shown in Diagram 5.2.

The names John and Mary have been replaced by a description of the jobs that they perform. The arrows represent the flow of data into, between, and out of functions. The boxes represent the functions performed, and the arrows represent the flow of data. The arrows into and out of a box are labelled, not with the names of documents, but with names of the data elements that flow along the arrows. Only the names of data elements that are used by a process (function) appear on arrows going into a box. No other labels will appear on an arrow. The two arrows that come out of the box with the function description *review date of last action* represent two functionally different types of data, the data to be ignored and the data to be passed to the function *determine action to be taken*. This function represents the examination of the accounts and a determination of the action to be taken. The arrow out of this box represents the specific data passed to other functions.

The completed diagram for the entire department, although it might be quite complicated, will allow the software technician to learn a considerable amount about the nature of the data that your department works with.

DIAGRAM 5.2

```
ACCOUNT NUMBER +
CREDIT LIMIT +
AMOUNT OVER LIMIT +
DATE OF LAST ACTION +          ┌─────────────────────┐
TYPE OF LAST ACTION            │  REVIEW DATE OF     │
          ────────────────────▶│  LAST ACTION        │
                               └─────────────────────┘

        INFORMATION FOR
◀──────────────────────────
      ACCOUNTS ACTED UPON       ACCOUNT NUMBER +
      WITHIN LAST THREE DAYS    CREDIT LIMIT +
                                AMOUNT OVER LIMIT +
                                DATE OF LAST ACTION +
                                TYPE OF LAST ACTION

                               ┌─────────────────────┐
                               │  DETERMINE ACTION   │
                               │  TO BE TAKEN        │
                               └─────────────────────┘

                                ACCOUNT NUMBER +
                                CREDIT LIMIT +
                                AMOUNT OVER LIMIT +
                                DATE OF CURRENT ACTION +
                                TYPE OF CURRENT ACTION
```

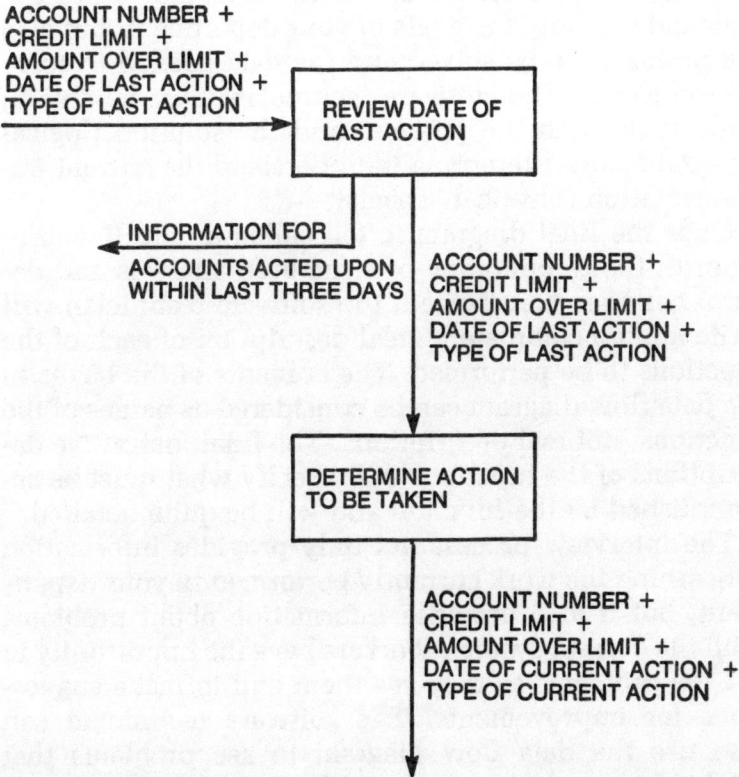

A diagram like Diagram 5.1 is quite physical in nature, meaning that it contains names of documents, people, and places. Since the names might change at any time and since the names are not central to the problem of understanding what data is needed and how it is used, it is preferable to transform such a diagram into one like Diagram 5.2. When we remove document, personal, and departmental names, we are closer to creating a logical diagram. Physical diagrams include names of documents, people, places, and considerations of how tasks are to be performed. Logical diagrams include names of data elements and functional descriptions, where a functional description is concerned with what must be accomplished by a task, not how it is to be accomplished. The conversion of a physical diagram into a logical diagram makes it easier for the software technician to understand not only the goals of your department, but also the problems to be solved and the data needed to solve the problems. The software technician must be able to understand both the problem and the solution (logical aspects) before attempting to understand the current implementation (physical aspects).

Once the final diagram (often called a *data flow diagram* in the terminology of structured analysis and design) has been constructed, the software technician will write a more complete logical description of each of the functions to be performed. The contents of the boxes in the data flow diagram can be considered as names of the functions, not real descriptions. The final, definitive descriptions of the functions will specify what must be accomplished by the function and will be quite detailed.

The interview process not only provides information concerning the work currently performed in your department, but it also provides information about problems with the current system. Workers have the opportunity to list the problems as they see them and to make suggestions for improvements. The software technician can also use the data flow diagram to see problems that might not have been mentioned by the workers. You and the software technician can then compile a list of problems (opportunities). You will then be able to analyze the problems, discover the nature and cause of the problems, and determine a list of possible solutions.

Among the actions that you might decide to take to solve any specific problem are: (1) reroute the flow of information, (2) modify a job description, i.e., perform certain functions in the department differently, add new functions, or delete some functions, (3) seek new sources of information, (4) provide the information in a different form, or (5) automate some functions.

The analysis skills of the software technician form the basis for any changes that you might wish to make. Be careful that you do not decide on the changes to be made before you understand the nature of the problems. Use the skills of the software technician to complement your own. Some of the skills that the technician has to offer you are: (1) gathering the data about how your department really works, (2) construction of the data flow diagram to make this data understandable, and (3) analysis of the diagram to help you understand the nature of the problems.

The technician can also offer some suggestions for improvement, but your skills are used to select the most feasible solutions offered by the technician, to add solutions of your own, and to gather the resources necessary to implement the chosen solutions.

You and the software technician must also gain a clear understanding of your personal needs as well as the needs of your department. Remember that your private information system will serve a number of functions:

1. Provide you with the specific information that you need to do your job the way that you want to do it.
2. Help you to reorganize your personal workload.
3. Help you to reorganize your department.
4. Save you time and energy.
5. Provide new information to you and your subordinates.
6. Provide current information in a better form for both you and your subordinates.
7. Monitor your critical success factors.
8. Monitor the critical success factors of some of your subordinates.
9. If possible, provide new and useful information to your superiors.

Once you and the software technician really understand your needs and the needs of your department, then you can start to take steps for improvement.

5.3 Design

A design is a logical solution to your problems and consists of a number of distinct steps.

5.3.1 A Logical Solution

A logical solution is worked out first. The logical solution specifies what must be accomplished in order to reach your personal goals and the goals that you set for your department. A logical solution may include a data flow diagram that incorporates the new data flows and functions.

5.3.2 A Preliminary Implementation

After the logical solution has been worked out, you must determine, to some degree, how the chosen solution will be implemented. Your descriptions of "what must be done" must be converted into descriptions of "how it will be done." You must be able to answer questions like: (A) What parts will be automated? (B) What kind of computer and modem will be used? and (C) What kind of system development and communciations software will be used?

5.3.3 More Specifics

The next step is to design the specifics of your private information system. You will need to decide which functions you can perform on the organization's computer (the one associated with the organization's information system) and which ones will be performed on your own microcomputer. The entire system must be designed as a whole, so that functions performed on one machine can easily be moved to another machine and so that new functions can easily be added. You will need this flexibility because you can never be sure of your access to the organization's information system. You may be told that you will be allowed access, and then the permission might be withdrawn at any time.

5.3.4 The Individual Parts of the Private Information System

The individual parts of your private information system, the part on the organization's computer and the part on your microcomputer, must then be designed. In some cases, the part of the private information system on the organization's computer will be a small, self-contained information system that interfaces with the organization's information system. It will have its own programs and data files, and some of the data for this part of the system will come from copies of organizational data. In other cases, this part of the private information system will be a collection of programs (there will be no files other than the standard organizational files) to be used with the query system, or merely an interactive use of the query system without any kind of programs. The specific design of this part of your private information system will depend upon: (A) the scope of the data that you are allowed access to, (B) the kind of access permitted, (C) permission to use your own programs, and (D) permission to have your own private files.

If permission is denied or if access is restricted, then you will need to rely more heavily on the standard system facilities, such as the query system, rather than on your own personal additions to the system.

The part of the private information system that will reside in your microcomputer will offer the most flexibility, since you have complete control over it and do not need permission to use it. It is for this machine that you will need the system development and communications software. I recommend that you perform the analysis and a good percentage of the design (at least 50 percent) before you decide which software development package(s) to use. This will allow you to select the software development system to fit the project, rather than force you to restrict your project to match the system development software.

I strongly recommend that you complete a major portion of the design before a software development system is selected. This will ensure that the software will be suitable for the application.

5.3.5 Analysis and Design Techniques

A number of different analysis and design techniques are available for the construction of your private information system. They are not all equivalent. The two common types are the *application-oriented* approach and the *structured* approach. In the application-oriented approach, the outputs (reports) are determined first, and the data files are constructed specifically to match the reports. At first glance this approach seems to have the advantage of being goal directed, but there are a number of severe disadvantages.

A. If you make significant changes in your reports, then you may have to redesign your files.
B. When this approach is used, a number of files may be logically related, but you may not be able to associate records in one file with related records in another file. If this situation occurs, then your files may have to be redesigned.
C. A file redesign may require that you make a number of changes in the programs that use the changed files.

In general, the application-oriented approach tends to lead to a design that is not flexible enough for a modern type of information system.

The structured approach was made popular by Tom DeMarco in his excellent book, *Structured Analysis and System Specifications*, Prentice-Hall, 1979. This approach treats the data, not the reports, as the most important feature of an information system. In fact, the analysis techniques, such as the data flow diagram, introduced above are structured analysis techniques. In this approach, the data files are determined from the nature of the data itself, not from how the data is expected to be used. This means that the data files are, for the most part, constructed independently of the expected manner of usage, so changes in programs and reports should not cause significant changes in the data files. The data files are then insulated from changes in programs and reports, so a change in a program will not cause a change in a file which might then cause changes in a number of different programs. In addition, files developed under the structured approach are integrated. Thus, if records in one file are logically related to records in another file, then you will be able to preserve this relationship and use it in your private information system. It is the ability to preserve and use relationships between data, and the ability to add new relationships without changing the basic structure of your files that will make your private information system truly flexible. If your files are not designed to allow you to add new relationships at will, then your private information system will probably not be flexible enough for your purposes. Remember that your understanding and the understanding of your software technician will evolve over a period of time. If your system is not flexible enough, then a change in understanding may lead to a major redesign of the entire system. You simply don't have the time, energy, and money to redesign your system a number of times.

Be wary of design techniques that force the data files to match the expected reports (outputs).

In the structured approach, the data flow diagram that will represent your private information system is usually obtained by modifying the data flow diagram for your current information system. The file design is usually obtained by creating one large (conceptual) file with all of the data in it that you will need, and then breaking up this large file into a collection of interrelated files that have the following characteristics:

A. Each file has just one type of record in it.
B. A record describes just one type of object. For example, a record might contain information concerning an employee and would not contain any information that does not specifically pertain to the employee.

C. No two different types of records describe the same type of object.

The purpose of these characteristics is to ensure that the files are as flexible as possible.

Once the files have been constructed and the programs have been designed, minor modifications are often made to the files in order to speed up certain functions. In any system a number of functions will be used frequently. A general rule of application systems is that a function performed frequently must be fast. Sometimes programs can be made fast by techniques like the careful duplication of data in the files. This means that the files may have to be "fine tuned" in order to make the time required for the operation of the system acceptable. These modifications may affect the criteria for a good file design as given above, i.e., we may modify our files so that they do not have a perfect structure, but we accept this as a fact of life in order to speed up some of the functions in our system. These modifications may cause trouble for us if we are not careful. For example, we may, because of duplication of data, have data in one record that is supposed to exactly match data in another record, but it doesn't. Inconsistency of this type must be eliminated either because the system carefully controls it or because we use the system in such a way as to guarantee that it will not happen. I prefer to have the application system enforce this for me, rather than rely on careful usage of the system by a number of people. There are often trade-offs in computing: you accept a small disadvantage in order to gain a big advantage.

5.3.6 Changing the Original Design

Once the design has been completed, the programming can begin. When the programming gets underway, you will find that more analysis and design will need to be performed. This is a consequence of the evolutionary nature of understanding. As the system is being programmed and pieces of it start to get used, both you and your software technician will discover that parts of the system must be deleted, modified, or added to. It is not possible to actually complete all of the analysis, then all of the design, and then all of the programming. You will find that there will be a cyclical repetition of these three functions, but with a well-designed system (and structured analysis and design techniques usually produce a well-designed system) the required changes are relatively easy to implement.

A good software technician will design your system so that it will be easy to modify as your understanding and the understanding of the software technician evolves.

5.3.7 Documentation and Changes to the Specifications

Make sure that there is reasonable documentation for the system before the programming begins. Don't let the software technician try to carry all of the specifications for the system in his or her head. Get the specifications written down. You will find that there will be a number of changes to the original design, and changes to the changes, and so forth. If you don't record the original design and document each of the changes, then the design for the private information system will become impossible to keep straight. You will remember the design one way, the technician will remember it another way, and you probably will both be wrong. Even worse, changes in the design might lead to programs that should work together but don't.

Whenever changes are made to the system, the software technician will need to inform you of the consequences, and you will have to decide whether or not to go ahead with the changes. The general rule of thumb is:

earlier in the project that changes are made, the smaller the impact upon the system. If you make a large number of changes during or after the programming stage, the system may become unstable. Things that used to work correctly now mysteriously don't work any more.

Even worse, things that used to work correctly now work correctly most of the time, but nobody knows why they sometimes work and why they sometimes don't.

5.3.8 A Timetable

Do not expect a definitive timetable from the software technician until a major portion of the design has been completed. If you attempt to hurry into the programming without a careful analysis and design, either the system that you are building will never be completed or it will take significantly longer. Go carefully and slowly during analysis and design so that you can go quickly during the programming. Diagrams 5.3 and 5.4 will give you an indication of what will happen if you try to rush through the analysis and design too quickly:

DIAGRAM 5.3 Programming May Continue for a Long Time

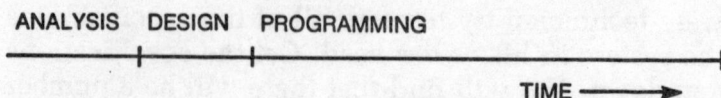

ANALYSIS   DESIGN   PROGRAMMING

TIME ———►

DIAGRAM 5.4 Programming Is Performed Quickly

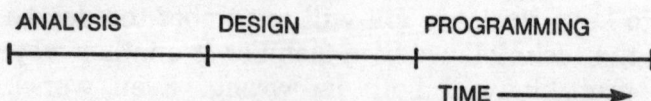

ANALYSIS   DESIGN   PROGRAMMING

TIME ———►

Devoting sufficient time to produce a good analysis and design will reduce the total amount of time required for the completion of your private information system.

5.4 Programming

Programming is a two-step process that involves the formulation of the specific algorithms from the design specifications and then the coding of the programs. The conversion of the specifications into the actual algorithms is not an easy task, and it usually requires a considerable amount of training and experience. The coding of the algorithms, i.e., writing the algorithms in a programming language, is easier than the conversion but still entails some difficulties. The overall design of your private information system should include a criteria for successful testing. The testing is performed each time a major portion of the programming has been completed and again after the entire system has been completed.

The transformation or conversion of the specifications for the functions into algorithms is usually performed using a process called *top-down design*. Top-down design involves a restatement of the original specifications, which are given in terms of what must be done, not how it must be done. The restatement refines the previous specifications or description, giving more information. Each restatement is in turn refined or restated, giving more information, until the original specifications have been transformed from a statement of "what must be done" into a collection of statements that specify "how it will be done." One rule for this stepwise refinement process is that if a decision about how something will be done can be delayed until the next step in the refinement process, it should be delayed. This defers any implementation decisions until the last possible point and leads to a more flexible program design. Since the decisions are made late instead of early in the program design, the consequences of any changes in the design of the programs are minimized. Notice that some of the philosophy associated with system design is also used in program design. The reason for this approach is to produce a flexible system and to produce programs that are themselves flexible. You should be aware by now that your software technician must be competent in three different areas: analysis, design, and programming. If the technician is not competent in any one of these areas, you will have major problems with your system.

The second part of programming is the encoding of the algorithms in a specific programming language. A specific coding technique (actually a philosophy) called *structured programming* should be used here. Structured programming means that a particular, rational discipline of programming is being used. The original algorithm is designed and coded so that the finished program to a great degree matches the pieces of the algorithm obtained from the stepwise refinement process. Collections of statements in the program are called *modules,* and, through the use of structured programming techniques, we wish to associate the following characteristics with our program and modules:

1. The modules should be small enough that we can understand each statement in the module and the purpose of the module.
2. We should be able to follow the logic of the program by starting with the first (the main) module and then following the references to the other modules. The references to modules should approximately match the parts of the stepwise refinement process. The stepwise refinement process produces a treelike or hierarchical structure, and the structure of the program should generally match this hierarchical structure.
3. The modules should have the property that there is one way to enter them and one way to leave them. Each module is like a room which has two doors. You can enter only through one door, you can exit only through the other door, and there are no other entrances or exits.

When programs are constructed with these and a few other characteristics, they are easier for the programmer to read and to debug. To *debug* a program means to remove errors until it meets the specifications and will run on the computer. Program debugging is facilitated by the techniques of structured programming, but almost all programs need to be debugged to some degree. One of the keys to easy debugging is the ability to understand what the program is really doing when it is run. Since structured programming makes programs easier to read and understand, it makes them easier to debug. There are two major kinds of errors in programs: syntactical and semantic errors. A syntax error occurs when the program contains a statement (instruction) that is not allowed in the chosen programming language. In this case, the program cannot be run. A semantic error occurs when the logic of the program is different from the desired logic. The first symptom of this type of error is when the program runs on the computer, but you get incorrect output or you get no output at all.

Three of the steps involved in programming are: conversion of the specifications for the programs into algorithms, translation of the algorithms into programs, and the testing of the programs.

The construction of good programs is a multistep process involving good specifications, good design, and good coding. If modern techniques are not used at each step, then a mediocre or poor program will be the result. This is one reason that you need a software technician with both good training and sufficient experience.

5.5 Testing

5.5.1 The Purpose of Testing

The purpose of testing is to determine if your system works correctly. Unfortunately, since the results of the test depend upon the choice of the data used for the test, testing can reveal the presence of errors in the system but not their absence. This means that no amount of testing can prove that the system is free of errors, but testing is still a useful process. In fact, testing is so useful that no system should ever be used without testing it first. In my experience, a careful selection of test data will reveal over 90 percent of the semantic (logical) errors in the programs. The remainder of the errors, if any, will appear after the system becomes operational.

There is one kind of error that should never happen

but always does. The data is entered into the system in a form that has not been anticipated, and the system handles it incorrectly. Consider the following example:

> The data must have a special code contained in it in order for the system to interpret the data correctly. The code appears in the data in positions 1, 2, and 3. The software technician is given a list of codes and is told that these are the only possible codes; no other code is possible. If the technician goes under the assumption that no other codes will ever be entered, then real trouble occurs when an incorrect code is entered.

A reasonable solution to this kind of problem is to make the system self-protecting. This means that data is checked for reasonableness and validity. Data is reasonable if it is within certain acceptable bounds, and it is valid if it has the correct form and is on the approved list. For example, personal property tax on an automobile might be reasonable if it is nonnegative and less than $200. The code that designates the type of automobile might be valid if it is one of the codes on the approved list. To make a program or system self-protecting, each piece of data entered should be checked for reasonableness and validity. Unfortunately, such tests can be both time-consuming and complex. Most software technicians will design their system and programs so that a number of the most obvious tests for reasonableness and validity are performed, but some tests are always missed. As the system is used over a period of time and as errors of this type occur, additional tests are added as necessary.

5.5.2 Types of Testing

The software technician will usually construct a main driver for the system first. The main driver is a program or module that will control all of the activities within the system. Recall that the top–down design of a program produces a hierarchical program structure. When complete software systems are designed using the same basic top–down principles, a hierarchical structure for all of the software results, and the main driver is at the top of the structure. The main driver serves a function in your private information system that is similar to the function of the operating system in your microcomputer. It asks "What do you want to do next?", interprets your response, and then attempts to satisfy your request. Since the main driver controls all of the activities of your private information system, it is appropriate to build it first.

As each new program or module is built by the software technician, it is inserted into the system. Data is specifically selected to test the newly inserted program or module. The data may have been selected before any part of the system was built, or it may have been selected after the last insert was constructed. The point here is that the data has been selected to specifically test the last insert. The kind of data that I like to use will test all of the functions from the main driver down the hierarchical path to and including the last program or module inserted. In this manner, all of the programs and modules in the hierarchical path are tested and the last insert is tested too. This gives me ample opportunity to test and retest programs and modules near the top of the hierarchical structure.

Within each program or module there are a number of statements (sentences) in the programming language. Not only should each statement be tested, but the different combinations of statements should also be tested. Let's say, for example, that a program contains a decision of the form: If you decide one way, then do A—else do B. In this type of situation the software technician will need to test the program with two different sets of data in order to verify that: (1) the decision works correctly, (2) the module named A works correctly, and (3) the module named B works correctly.

Note that if there are two decisions in a row, then four different sets of data might be necessary in order to test all possible combinations of decisions. If there are three decisions, then the software technician might need to use eight different sets of data. In general, if there are n decisions, then it might be necessary to use two raised to the power n sets of data to thoroughly test the program. You can see why testing can be a tedious and time-consuming process, and why it is seldom done in a manner that will prove that the program works correctly.

An approach that I have used when I build systems is to select the data carefully so that it contains every situation that I can think of and write the program to catch and report any other situation. This allows me to test the inserted program with a relatively small number of different sets of data, cuts down on the total time that it takes to perform the testing, and still provides a reasonable test.

The parts of the private information system are usually tested by the software technician using a relatively small amount of data. This speeds up the total testing procedure and makes it possible to quickly verify the results of the test. The goal of this type of testing is to make the system as error-free as possible, recognizing that some errors will still remain. The assumption is that a large percentage of the errors will be removed by this type of testing and that the remainder of the errors can be removed after the system is turned over to the users.

Once the users receive the system, they should perform their own tests using a relatively small amount of operational data. Assume that you want your private information system to keep track of 100 transactions a day for you. You might start with 10 transactions a day, verifying each day that the system works as expected. As errors are found and corrected, you might increase the number of transactions handled each day by your private information system, until it works correctly under a full load. The reason for starting with a small amount of data and then gradually increasing it is to gain control over the testing phase. You must have enough data to verify that the system really works but use an amount of data that is small enough to be easy to handle. You must be able to make several test runs of the system in a reasonable amount of time, and you must be able to rapidly verify the correctness of the results of the individual tests. The testing by the users of the system is a stepwise process using gradually increasing amounts of operational data. *Warning:* Make sure that your system is thoroughly tested before you use the results that it produces. If you use incorrect data, then your project will probably fail and you might look foolish to your superiors.

The users of your private information system might have an opportunity to test individual parts of the system as they are developed, or they might have to wait until the entire system is built. I have used both techniques, and they appear to be equally successful. When the system is first tested with operational data, any of the following might arise:

1. Some parts of the system might be too time-consuming and cumbersome.
2. Some of the individual programs are too slow or do not work correctly.
3. The reports are incorrect, are hard to read, contain too much data, or contain too little data.
4. The instructions for the use of the system are not clear or are misleading.
5. The system has not been used as expected, some errors have occurred, and the users don't know what to do.
6. Parts of the system do not function as expected.
7. Some functions are missing.
8. Some cosmetic changes are necessary to make the system easier to use.

You and the other members of your department will not only want to know that the system works correctly, you will also want a system that is economical, easy to use, gives you the desired functions (power), and matches the way that you want to do things. Testing is your way of finding out what the system does and if you like it. This type of testing is often called *acceptance testing*. In the commercial market, once a system has passed the acceptance test phase, the users are stuck with the system as it is and must pay an additional amount for any more changes. You will not be in this situation unless you acquire the services of a software technician at a fixed dollar amount for the project. If the software technician works for you on a regular salaried basis (this is what I recommend), then acceptance testing merely means that the system does what you expect it to do at the current time, and no monetary commitment is associated with successful acceptance testing.

> You must personally assume the responsibility for the final testing of your private information system.

5.6 After the Testing

Once the private information system has been put into operation, you will find a number of reasons to change it. Some of the changes will occur as you discover additional errors in the system. At this point, the number of errors that you find should be relatively small and decrease further over a period of time. As your understanding of what a private information system can do for you and for your department grows, you will probably want to add more functions to your system. If the system was well designed to begin with, the required modifications and the addition of more functions should be a relatively easy task, but you may occasionally find modifications or additions that require major changes in the system. Examine the consequences of these changes and additions very carefully. You really don't want a major redesign and reprogramming effort unless the current design isn't sufficient and can't be fixed easily. If you find that a system needs to be completely redesigned, this may be indication of a poor design by the software technician. If you want a superior private information system, employ a superior software technician and invest a sufficient amount of your own time to make sure that the system is what you want.

Use both the acceptance testing and operational phases to fine tune your system. Don't be afraid to recommend changes as you see the need for them, but listen to the technician's warnings if the system starts to become unstable. If the changes really are necessary and if the changes will make the system unstable (and this can happen even if you have hired the world's best software technician), then you may want the technician to perform an analysis of your private information system to determine its current state. The analysis should be performed just like the analysis of the original situation was. In most cases, if the private information system was designed using modern techniques, then this analysis will lead to minor redesign and reprogramming efforts, saving you from having to build another private information system to replace your current one.

The analysis of your private information system should probably be done on a periodic basis anyway. It should be part of your master plan to measure your progress and to determine if you are moving toward your goals as planned. I estimate that a periodic evaluation of your private information system (carried out primarily by you and your software technician) will increase the effectiveness of the system by at least 50 percent.

5.7 Other Sources of Information

The two primary sources of information will be the organization's information system and the information that your department can independently gather, but there may be additional sources available. The greater the number of sources of applicable information, especially if the information is computerized, the easier it will be to complete your projects. Other managers in your organization may have private information systems and may be willing to exchange data. The data can be transferred from one microcomputer in a number of ways:

1. If you and another manager are using the same communications software, it may be possible to transfer large amounts of data directly from one machine to another using a simple cable that connects the two machines.

2. If you can create files for your own use on the organization's computer, you can send data from one microcomputer to the organization's computer and then send the data from the organization's computer to the other microcomputer. If you use this technique, make sure that the data gets transferred correctly; even a small amount

of interference on the communication line to or from the organization's computer can cause problems with the data.

3. If you are not allowed access to the organization's computer for this purpose, you might be able to use a different computer for the same purpose.

4. Modest amounts of data can be copied to a floppy disk. If your computer uses the same disk format, then you can read the disk directly. If the format is different, you might be able to obtain a special program to read disks of other formats directly on your own machine. Your software technician may be acquainted with such software. If you are using an IBM XT or a compatible machine, problems of this type will be simplified.

Other sources of data might include commercial and federal databanks. The commercial databanks are usually easier to access and provide the data in a form that is much easier to use. Once you try to get data from sources outside of your own company, the probability of the usefulness of the data rapidly diminishes.

5.8   Other Sources of Software

Up to now we have thought of the software technician as the individual responsible for writing all of the programs that you will need. In some cases, it may be possible to purchase software at a reasonable price that will perform some of the tasks that you want done. The advantages of this type of software are:

1. It is usually cheaper to purchase existing software than it is to develop it yourself. If the saving is significant, you may then have enough money to perform a number of additional functions, functions that you originally thought you couldn't do.

2. It usually takes less time to purchase software than to develop it yourself. The time savings might give you an advantage over others in the organization who might be trying to solve the same problem.

The disadvantages of this type of software are:

1. The software was written by someone other than your software technician. The problems that can result from this are:
   A. The software doesn't interface properly with other parts of your private information system.
   B. No one knows how the software really works, so it cannot be changed to fit your individual needs, errors in the software cannot be easily corrected (if they can be corrected at all), and you might not have confidence in the techniques used.
2. There is no way to judge the quality of the software before you use it. Since there are so many software packages on the market for microcomputers, you might obtain one that is very good or one that is terrible. You certainly want all of the parts of your system to have the same high quality.

A good software technician can do some research to help you determine if there is good software on the market that already does some of what you want, and he or she can help you determine if the cost is reasonable. Once the software has arrived, the software technician can test it for you and help you to determine if it is reasonable to use it in an operational environment. Software technicians usually have a considerable amount of experience interpreting instructions that come with this kind of software. You would be surprised at how bad some of the instructions are, even the instructions for very good software.

5.9 Selecting a Software Technician

When you start your private information system, you will need a good software technician. I use the term *software technician* rather than programmer, because you will need someone with good skills in the analysis, design, and programming of information systems. The software technician will build and maintain the new information system for you on your own microcomputer and/or on your organization's computer.

When you start searching for someone to build your private information system for you, look for a professional. Do not expect to build an adequate system with someone who has had one or two classes in programming. You will need someone who has had both training and experience in building information systems and who is familiar with modern techniques for analysis, design, and programming. You wish to build an information system that is easy to use, flexible, powerful, and reasonably fast. People without reasonable training will not even be able to build such a system. People without experience will not be able to build either a fast or an easy-to-use system. Most colleges and universities provide adequate training in programming for a computer science or information systems major, but most of them still do not provide both adequate training and experience in the construction of information systems. Look for someone who has had actual (and successful) experience in building some kind of information system, preferably on microcomputers.

Such a person is not easy to find. You may have to interview a number of people to find just the one you want. Expect to pay a good salary for such a person. Do not try to use several inferior workers to do the work of one good one. I have seen organizations hire two or three mediocre people instead of one really good one, and the results were disastrous. You wish to demonstrate that you have what it takes to move into high-level management, and you need first-rate ideas and tools to do this. Don't cause future problems for yourself by trying to use inferior personnel. This applies to both the software technician and to the person that will enter the data for you. If the data that you use is not accurate and complete, it will surely cause you trouble. You may spend a considerable amount of time and energy working with the incorrect data before you realize your mistakes. You may even make a proposal or a presentation to your superiors based upon erroneous information.

Don't spend too much for a software technician, but don't try to spend too little either. If you use wages as a main criteria for selection, you could easily get just what you pay for—a second-rate job.

The ideal software technician will have each of the following characteristics:

1. At least a four-year degree (BS or BA, possibly a master's or a doctorate) in computer science or information systems.

2. Specific courses in the modern techniques of analysis, design, and programming of information systems, including structured analysis, structured design, and structured programming. Be flexible here, since the candidate may use different but equivalent techniques. Nevertheless, the candidate should know what each of these techniques are and be able to discuss them with you.

3. An in-depth knowledge of and experience with the common microcomputers, especially the IBM XT or compatible machines.

4. A knowledge of the common kinds of system development software available on microcomputers.

5. A knowledge of at least one kind of communications software available on microcomputers.

6. Previous experience in all phases of the construction of information systems. This does not mean just classroom exposure but actual experience. The candidate must be able to perform the functions of analysis, design, and programming, and must be able to do each one both independently and creatively.

7. Previous experience building a private information system is desirable but not necessary.

8. The candidate must be able to get along with the members of your department. This means that the candidate must have the basic social skills necessary for the required human interaction. In particular, the candidate

must not feel that he or she knows all that there is to
know about the construction of information systems or
about the work that your department does.

5.10 Data Entry

Since we are discussing the qualifications for a software
technician in this chapter, it seems appropriate to discuss the qualifications for another person who will be
associated with your private information system. In addition to a software technician, you will need to select
someone to enter the data into your private information
system. Be careful when choosing someone to enter data.
Typing and secretarial skills are seldom adequate for
correct and consistent data entry. In addition, if your private information system is ambitious, then the individual chosen to enter the data might need a considerable
amount of time to perform this task. Individuals who already have a work assignment in your organization will
seldom have free time for the additional duties of data
entry. They will look at the data entry assignment as an
extra burden, will resent the extra work, and will not do
an adequate job.

Do not assume that ordinary secretarial skills are sufficient for good entry of data.

Do not assume that you can add data entry responsibilities to the existing workload of an employee.

CHAPTER 6

Software Development Systems

6.1 Types of Files

Any system that allows you to write programs could be considered a software development system, so it is reasonable to examine the various types of development systems for advantages and disadvantages. It is possible to divide the software development systems into two main categories: those that are restricted to the use of the file manipulation facilities provided by the operating system and those that extend these operating system facilities.

Files may be accessed in three major ways: read only, write only, and for both reading and writing (read/write). The type of access to be used might be established at the time that the file is created or it might be established at the time that the user requests access to the file. In the first case, the type of access is fixed, i.e., only one type of access is possible. In the second case, it might be possible to change the type of access according to the needs of the users. In general, a file is opened in one of the three access modes, the file is then used for a period of time, and the file is then closed. In some cases, you may open and access a file in one mode, close the file, and then reopen the file and use it in another access mode.

When a file is accessed in read-only mode, the user may view (read) the data in the file but may not make any changes to the data, add any new data, or delete any existing data. The read-only mode is useful when you wish to allow access to the data but protect it from unauthorized or accidental changes.

When a file is accessed in write-only mode, a new file of the given name is always created. If there is a file in existence with the given name, then the data in that file is lost (discarded). If you wish to preserve the data in the file, you must copy it to a file of a different name before you open the file in write-only mode. A file that has been created in write-only mode may then be accessed, if desired, in read-only mode, after it has been closed and then reopened. The creation of a file in the write-only mode is useful in the situation when you wish to create a file that will be used for a short period of time, after which the contents will no longer be needed.

When a file is accessed in read/write mode, you may read from the file and you may write to the same file, without closing the file between different types of operations. In this case, writing to the file does not destroy the entire contents of the file. Changing existing data is usually a three-step process: obtain the desired data, view and make changes in the data, and then replace the old data with the new data. It is also possible to add new data to or delete existing data from this kind of file. A variation of the read/write access mode is the read/append mode. In this mode, it is possible to read a file in the ordinary manner, but it is also possible to add new data only to the end of the file.

Database and file management systems are extensions of or replacements for the file manipulation facilities offered through the operating system. They allow you to access the data in any of the modes described above, and they facilitate linking related records in different files together. The linking together of related records makes this kind of system powerful. You must be able to link records together to have a truly effective private information system.

Another way of categorizing files has to do with the manner of accessing specific records. The two major types of access to records are called *sequential* and *direct*, where direct is sometimes called *random*. The order of the records in a file that is organized sequentially is important, since access is performed in a record-by-record manner. If you are currently examining a record in the file and you wish to examine some other record in the file, then you must examine all of the records in between, obtaining the records and examining them to determine which one is the record that you want. Direct access does not require that you examine all intervening records. In order to access a record in direct access mode, you obtain or calculate the address (location) of the desired record, and then go directly to the desired location.

Both sequential and direct access modes are important. Some processes (programs) are efficient if access is sequential but inefficient if access is direct. Others are efficient if access is direct but inefficient if access is sequential. In addition, the efficiency of the process may vary with the percentage of records accessed. Thus, a process may be efficient if sequential access is used and the percentage of records to be accessed is large, and the same process may be efficient if direct access is used and the percentage of records to be accessed is small. Any selection of a software development system should provide you with the opportunity to create files that can be accessed either sequentially or directly. This means that you should be able to create a file that can be accessed sequentially at one time, and then the same file can be accessed directly at another time. Make sure that your software development system has this facility.

Your software development system must allow you to create files that can be accessed either sequentially or directly.

6.2 Languages

Most of the standard (popular) programming languages, such as ALGOL, BASIC, COBOL, FORTRAN, and PASCAL, do not usually provide the facilities to link records together. In some cases, these languages have been extended to include this facility, but I personally have found this type of extension quite hard to use. I therefore recommend that you do not use a common language like ALGOL, BASIC, COBOL, FORTRAN, or PASCAL that has been extended to provide the facility to link records together as part of the software development system for your private information system.

I prefer to use software development systems that have their own specialized language. Such a language has the power to perform most or all of the functions that the common languages do (at least the ones that we would be interested in) but also provides an interface to the files that is both powerful and simple. In this type of language, the ability to store, access, and manipulate the data is built right into the language itself, making the use of the system considerably easier than a system that uses a popular language that has been extended. Another advantage of this type of language is that nonprogrammers can learn to use some of the facilities of the language, since they are so similar to a query facility. It is not expected that you will be a proficient programmer, but it is nice to know that you will be able to use parts of the language yourself if you need to.

When you select a software development system, look for a language that is easy to use. Remember that an extension of a popular programming language may be quite difficult to program in.

6.3 Compilers and Interpreters

After programs are written, they must be executed by the computer. If the program is first translated into a language that the computer can understand, then we say that it has been compiled. A *compiler* is a system program that takes your application program and translates or converts it into a program in the language of the machine. An *interpreter* is a system program that has the ability to directly execute your program without first converting it into the language of the computer. Some software development systems perform a process similar to compilation, but the result is not a program in the language of the machine—it is a program in an intermediate language called P-code. The P-code program is then interpreted by another development system program. As you can see, there are a variety of techniques to execute your application programs, but techniques used on your own computer will depend upon the software development system that you select. Your software development system will probably do one of the following: compile to machine code, compile to P-code and then interpret it, or directly interpret your application program. Each of these three types of execution mode (and there are a few others not mentioned here) have their advantages and disadvantages:

1. Compilation: fast execution speed, but few helps for debugging and tracking down errors.
2. Interpretation: slow execution speed, but very good helps for debugging and tracking down errors.
3. Compilation to P-code followed by interpretation of the P-code: moderate execution speed and reasonable helps for debugging and tracking down errors.

Most software development systems now on the market offer you only one choice: they either compile, directly interpret, or compile to P-code. If you desire to use a particular name brand of software development system, you are usually stuck with whatever type of execution is provided by the manufacturer. Since there is usually only one kind of execution mode available with a particular software development system, you may decide to reject a system for your own use, if there is another one that offers the same basic facilities but has a more desirable execution mode. The desirability of the execution mode is directly dependent upon your own needs. No one mode will be appropriate for all systems.

> Choose a type of system based upon your individual
> needs. A compiler will produce a fast system. An inter-
> preter will produce good error messages and help in de-
> bugging programs.

6.4 Types of Software Facilities

The basic software facilities (functions or services) that
you will need for the development of your private information system are: (1) an editor, (2) a compiler or interpreter, (3) a query facility, and (4) communications software.

The major purpose of the editor is to allow you to
write programs, and it is similar to a word processing
program. There are a number of good editors on the market, so you have a number to select from. When I write
programs, I like to use WordStar. It is a good word processing program that has all of the facilities that I like,
both as a word processor and as an editor. Nevertheless,
other editors are equally good.

The compiler or interpreter will be part of the software
development system that you purchase. Compilers and in-
terpreters have been previously discussed in this chapter.

The query facility is a part of the software development system. When you purchase the system, make sure
that a good query facility is included. There are two
types of query facility: one that is contained as a part of
the system and one that has been added to it. I greatly
prefer the kind that is contained within the system itself
for a number of reasons: (1) it is usually cheaper, (2) it is
easier to use, (3) it interfaces nicely with other parts of
the system, and (4) the language of the programs and the
language of the query facility will be similar, making it
easier for the programmer to keep them straight.

With your query facility, you, as a nonprogrammer,
should be able to perform all of the tasks which follow. If
you can't, then the query facility is not powerful
enough.

1. View and optionally print the contents of records in any of the files used in your private information system.
2. Select records and fields using a complex selection criteria for the purpose of viewing, deleting, or modifying them.
3. Make changes to the same field in all records or to a number of fields in several records.
4. Print simple reports.

The communication software should provide you with the ability to communicate both with a mainframe computer and with other microcomputers. The two modes of communication are the dumb and intelligent modes. Dumb communication treats one of the two parties as an ordinary terminal. When a computer is treated as a terminal, no effort is made by the sender to verify that the data has been correctly received. Intelligent communication means that each of the two parties can pass information to the other about the status of their ability to send and receive data, and they can mutually determine if the data has been received correctly.

Intelligent communication can take place between any two computers, as long as compatible software is being used on each of the two machines. The communication between two microcomputers is usually made intelligent by running the identical or similar (compatible) communications programs on each machine. The two programs can then "talk" to each other. A data file is broken up into pieces called *blocks*, and the blocks are sent one at a time. Each time a block is sent, the receiving computer informs the sending computer whether or not the block has been correctly received. There are two common techniques in use to determine if a block has been correctly received:

1. *Technique number one:* Each block is sent twice and the second block is compared with the first block by the receiver. If the two blocks do not agree (are not identical), then the block is sent twice again. If necessary, the process is repeated either until it is successful or until a maximum number of repetitions has been accomplished.

2. *Technique number two:* A block and a description of the block are sent. The description of the block, called a *checksum,* is based upon the actual data in the block. When the block is received, the receiving communications software computes its own checksum from the data block itself and compares the newly computed checksum with the one sent to it. If they agree, then the block is considered to have been successfully received. If they differ, then the block and the checksum are transmitted again.

Each of these two techniques have their advantages and disadvantages. Sending the block twice is slow but highly accurate. Sending each block once, with a checksum, is fast since the checksum is usually very short, but it is possible for a block to be received incorrectly and still have the checksum computed by the receiving computer match the checksum sent by the sending computer. Nevertheless, the checksum technique is accurate enough that most communications software packages use it.

Intelligent communication between a microcomputer and a mainframe is possible, but the techniques used are slightly different. The machine language of the microcomputer and the machine language of the mainframe are usually different, so the same communication package cannot easily be used on the two machines. One way to solve this problem is to run a program on the mainframe to emulate a microcomputer, i.e., to make it look like a microcomputer. Then the same communications software can be used on both machines. Another technique is to use a communications software program on the mainframe that has a standard interface, being able to "talk" to the communications software on the microcomputer. In any case, intelligent communication is preferable to dumb communication because we always want to verify, in some manner, that the data has been correctly received. Most communication between a microcomputer and a mainframe takes place over telephone lines. The interference (noise) on such lines is often bad enough to change the contents of the data transmission (introduce errors in the data), in much the same way that interference is introduced into radio, television, and ordinary telephone speech communications. Dumb communication does not detect and attempt to correct the errors in the transmission, but intelligent communication does. If you have very "clean" (interference-free) communications between your microcomputer and the mainframe, then you do not need to have intelligent communications, but it is still desirable since it will catch the occasional error. Even if you use very clean telephone lines, you will find that occasional errors occur in the data.

> Intelligent communication is required if the line from your microcomputer to the organization's computer is noisy.

6.5 Types of Software Packages

The basic types of software packages are: (1) editors, (2) communications software, and (3) the programming and data manipulation system. Editors and communication software have been discussed above. I have included the programming and the data manipulation parts of the software development system together, since you will essentially always find them in the same package.

The programming and data manipulation system are the heart of the software development system. Working together, they allow you to structure the data files so that you can link records together, and they allow you to enter, store, access, manipulate, and report the data. For simplicity, in the following, we will simply call the programming and data manipulation system the development system.

There are a number of different types of development systems on the market. Each one is designed to solve a certain class of problems, and some of them solve the same kind of problems but in different ways. The kinds of problems that they address include:

1. Simplified entry of data,
2. Production of reports,
3. Ordinary computations and manipulations of data,
4. Specialized types of computations and manipulations,
5. Drawing pictures, diagrams, and graphs (graphics),
6. Specialized, integrated data display,
7. Planning and coordination, and
8. Data retrieval.

Each of these types of problems is quite important and will be addressed in turn.

The Simplified Entry of Data

The entry of data is both time consuming and error prone. Since the correct entry of the data is so important to any information system, some software development systems offer facilities that simplify both the actual entry of the data and the verification of the correctness of the data's form. The type of entry that I prefer is called *full-screen entry*. When this type of entry is used, a blank document is presented on the screen of the microcomputer. A document is blank if it has the form of a document but the data has not been entered yet. The cursor is moved about the screen for you as you enter each piece of data. For example, assume that you are entering data for an employee, and that the data to be entered includes: last name, first name, National Insurance number, telephone number, date hired, and current salary. When full-screen entry is used, a document similar to the one in Diagram 6.1 will be presented on the screen.

When the blank document is presented on the screen, the areas for the entry of data are often marked in some fashion. The areas may be delimited, as by colons (:), may appear on the screen with a different intensity, or may appear with a different colour. The cursor is then positioned in the first field to be filled in. If you completely fill a field, for example, with the National Insurance number, the cursor will automatically be moved for you to the next field to be filled in. If your data does not completely

DIAGRAM 6.1

SSN: :

Last name: First name: :

Telephone: :

Date hired: /   /   :

Current salary: :

fill the field, you may then advance to the next field by striking the return or entry keys of your microcomputer. It is also common to allow the user to move the cursor around the screen to correct errors. For example, if you notice while entering the field labelled *date hired* that the social security number has been entered incorrectly, you may move the cursor back to the field labeled SSN and then make the appropriate corrections. If you find out that a field has been entered incorrectly after the document has been completed, then you may recall it to the screen, with all of the data that you have already entered in this document displayed for you, to make the desired corrections.

When you are entering the data for individual fields, it is checked for both correctness of type and for reasonableness. For example, full-screen data entry will not let you enter a letter in a field that is supposed to hold a number. Reasonableness can be determined in at least three different ways: the data must be within the correct range, it must be one of the items on an approved list, or it must satisfy a special criteria previously entered into the system. An example of a special criteria is: if the employee works in a certain department, then the four-digit telephone number (extension number) must start with a specified digit. The special criteria might involve data within the record currently being entered, data stored in a program, or data stored in a separate file. The flexibility and power of a full-screen data entry system will save days or even weeks of difficult programming, will reduce the total cost of data entry by a considerable amount, and will greatly increase the reliability of the data. In most cases, it will also reduce the total amount of time that is required for entry of data. This might be important to you, if a large volume of data will be entered into your private information system.

> Look for software development systems that facilitate the data entry process.

The Production of Reports

There are two major ways to produce reports: use detailed programs or use special reporting facilities. Since programs that produce reports are like any other programs, except that they are specifically designed to print reports, the code written to produce the reports is called *procedural*. When special reporting facilities are used, one merely describes what the report is supposed to look like and how some of the computations are to be performed. The software development system then uses your descriptions (not your programs) to produce the report. This type of code is called *descriptive*.

The advantage of procedural code for the production of reports is that you can produce essentially any kind of report that you want. In some cases special help is available to design the format of the report, but the programmer bears by far the major responsibility for the program. The disadvantage of procedural code is the large amount of detailed programming. It takes time to write the program for a report, especially the structure of the report. For example, the report title must be centred on the paper, any columns of data must have headings, and columns of numbers usually have totals. When procedural code is used, the programmer must also take the responsibility for determining certain clerical tasks, such as advancing to the top of the next page before printing a detail line and the printing of page numbers. The spacing of output on the page and the clerical tasks can take an unexpectedly large amount of time.

The advantage of descriptive code is that the spacing and arranging of the output on the page is simplified, and the clerical tasks are often automated. The use of descriptive code can save an extraordinary amount of programming time, and the descriptive code is usually much easier to debug in case there are any errors. The disadvantage is that descriptive code is often highly stylized, so you may be able to get only one kind of report. A number of people do not like to use descriptive code in a professional programming environment, but I really like to use it when I can. I think that the time savings more than outweigh any of the potential disadvantages.

If your development system allows you to write descriptive code to print reports, then it is said to have a report writer capability. If your system has this capability, don't be afraid to use it. It will mean that your private information system will be developed more quickly.

If your selection of a software development system allows you to use descriptive code (a report writer) for reports, you may be able to save some programming time.

Ordinary Computations and Manipulations of Data

In every private information system there will be a need for ordinary mathematics, for simplified logic, and for the manipulation of character strings. Your development system should at least allow you to perform the arithmetic operations: addition, subtraction, multiplication, division, and exponentiation. You may have additional needs that are specific to your own situation, such as complex arithmetic. If your needs are great enough, then you may find that you cannot use some of the development systems on the market. Your system should allow you to specify conditions using the logical operators: and, or, not. If these are not available, then the programming may become unnecessarily difficult. For many private information systems, the ability to manipulate character strings (nonnumeric data) is a must. The character string functions, among other things, allow you to obtain pieces of a character string and to concatenate two character strings to form a new one. Some systems have essentially no character string manipulation functions, and others have an abundance of them. Remember that you will have to select a development system to meet your needs, so perform a good analysis of your needs first, and then select a development system that will satisfy your needs.

Specialized Types of Computations and Manipulations

You may be working in an environment where the tasks that you have to perform are both highly stylized and environment specific. For example, in a savings and loan environment you would probably like to have functions that would help you compute various kinds of interest, discount rates, and points. It is not uncommon to have a specialized kind of computation associated with a job, so look in the development system for the ability to perform the kinds of computations that are normally associated with your particular job. There are two ways that specialized computations can be performed: the first is to use functions already available within the system, and the second is to build the functions yourself. If the functions are already available, then many of the programming tasks will be simplified. If the software technician has to build the functions, make sure that the necessary building blocks are in the language of the software development system. In some cases you may need logarithms and exponentiation, but these may not be available in every development system.

Drawing Pictures, Diagrams, and Graphs

The ability to draw pictures, diagrams, and graphs requires specialized software and often requires specialized hardware. Some microcomputers do not have the ability to draw on the screen, so make sure that yours does, if you need this capability. To produce permanent copies of pictures, diagrams, or graphs, you might be able to use a dot matrix printer with graphics capability, a plotter (a special graphics output device), or a special camera to take pictures of your screen. If you choose a dot matrix printer for your private information system, I recommend that you make it one with graphics capability. The difference in cost between a printer without the graphics capability and one with it is minimal, and you might find the graphics capability highly useful. A plotter might cost you as much as £1,000, so I recommend that you purchase one only if you need the enhanced output or color capabilities. A cost effective alternative to a plotter is an instant camera with a special hood attachment. You can place the hood against the screen and take a picture of the screen with the camera. Since the film develops within a minute, you will be able to see if the picture on the screen was properly captured.

The ability to produce graphics requires specialized graphics software. This software may come as part of your microcomputer system software or it may be available within your development system. If you need graphics, make the software vendor demonstrate that it will work both with your screen and with your printer. I once purchased a graphics package for use with my computer and printer. The producer of the package stated in writing that I would be able to use my printer to produce graphics. I tried it, and of course it didn't work. When I called the producer of the software I was told that I needed to have a special £90 chip (integrated circuit) installed in my printer before I could produce the desired graphical output. Make sure, if you can, that any software will work before you purchase it.

The most common kinds of graphical outputs are: (1) line drawings, (2) graphs and plots, and (3) smooth shaded pictures. Most of the software and hardware that will produce graphical output will produce line drawings, graphs, and plots. Smooth shaded pictures look like actual photographs and so are highly desirable, but the necessary hardware and software is, at the present time, quite expensive. I suspect that line drawings, graphs, and plots will be sufficient for most private information systems.

The ability to produce line drawings, graphs, and plots is highly desirable since it will make your reports and presentations more understandable and more professional looking. Even if you think that you will not need this capability, see if you can obtain it for a minimal cost. You might be very glad that you did.

Graphics may be a feature that you need. If so, look for a system that will provide you with this feature. Also make sure that your printer is suitable for graphics, if you do not expect to use a plotter.

Specialized, Integrated Data Display

There are some situations where ordinary reports and graphical displays do not allow the user to display the data in the desired manner. The situation may be ordinary or it may be job specific. Consider the situation where you wish to display integrated data of the following type:

You wish to display the projected cash flow on a monthly basis. You decide to produce a report in the format depicted in Diagram 6.2.

This kind of a report does not seem to fit the format of the report writer very well, and you would probably like to have some additional characteristics. Since this is a projected cash flow report, you would like to do some experimentation. You would like to see what the results are if you make changes in the values of any of the receipts or disbursements, and you would like to see the effects of the changes immediately on the screen. In addition, you would like some extra help in setting up the report. Since the columns for all of the months of the year have exactly the same format, you would like to define the calculations for

DIAGRAM 6.2

Projected Cash Flow for the Year

	JAN	FEB	MAR	APR
Receipts:				
Cash, beginning				
A/R collections				
Note additions				
Long-term debt				
Cash available	___	___	___	___
Disbursements:				
Property and plant				
Accounts payable				
Accrued expenses				
Note repayment				
Long-term debt				
Income taxes				
Cash disbursed	___	___	___	___
Ending cash				

January and be able to use the same calculations for all of the remaining columns of the same type.

The above example illustrates needs that are not easily met either by ordinary programs or by the report writer. In this case, an automated spreadsheet would be appropriate. The automated spreadsheet is an example of a specialized, integrated data display. It is specialized in the sense that special functions are built into the system, for example, the ability to duplicate the definition of one column to form the definition for another column. It is also integrated in the sense that a change of data in one place on the display causes corresponding changes in all of the places where that specific data is used. In the spreadsheet given in Diagram 6.2, a change, for example, in the accounts receivable collections (*A/R collections*) would automatically change both the *cash available* and the *ending cash* figures.

Planning and Coordination

One of the tasks of the manager is to plan and to monitor the progress made during the implementation of the plan. Progress toward milestones and the consumption of resources, including time, money, and materials, must both be carefully monitored. Some plans are so complex, i.e., parts of the plan are so intricately connected to each other, that a delay in one small part of the plan may cause a major delay in the entire project. A common approach to this problem is to computerize the monitoring and the reporting of the project, taking special note of the critical paths. Reports are produced on a regular basis that indicate both the critical paths and any deviation from the expected schedule.

Since a large number of individual tasks are often associated with such a project, the amount of input and the length of reports can be truly staggering. I suspect the reason so many automated job tracking systems of this type are difficult to use is that the sheer volume of both the input and the output is so large. This type of system is available on microcomputers and may be valuable in providing you with highly specialized information.

If you choose to use such a system of your own, it is probably because you are not getting the kind of information that you need from the organization's information system. In a number of books on management principles, this type of system is presented as a cure for many of the problems associated with the management of large projects. My experience leads me to believe that reliance on such a system for the monitoring of a large project is fraught with a number of dangers. This type of system sounds good and looks good—until you are the one that is trying to use it. Again, the sheer volume of input and output is the major cause of the problem.

If you are planning to use such a system, I strongly recommend that you use it cautiously and with some restrictions.

1. Assign a number of new people to the task of gathering and entering the data. Do not assume that you can use such a system without additional resources (people).

In many cases, the use of an automated job tracking system requires more people than performing the same task manually. The payback, if there is one, will be in advance warning of problems.

2. Do not attempt to produce all of the reports provided by the system. The volume of output may be so great that you will not have time to review all of the reports and to take corrective action when necessary. Plan how you will monitor the project in advance, rather than rely on the automated system to spot all of the problems for you. Remember that the system will be written to be general in nature. It is written so that it can be used in a wide variety of situations; and it will therefore produce a number of reports, a significant percentage of which will either be marginal in utility or of no use to you at all. Examine the critical paths in the project and use the system to monitor these paths. Do not rely on the addition of personnel to the project at the last minute to keep it on schedule. The rule of thumb is that the later you add people to a project, the higher the probability will be that you will extend, not shorten, the amount of time required to complete the project. This rule not only applies to the project as a whole, but it also applies to the individual tasks in the project, especially to the critical tasks. Use this type of system to provide as much advance notice of problems as you can get. Notification of a problem after the fact is considerably less useful than notification of the problem before it gets serious.

3. Allow a sufficient time delay for the entry, processing, and reporting of the data. Too many managers assume that automated job tracking systems are fast enough to provide advance warning of problems, just because they are using a computer. You must carefully plan the entire operation, estimate the delays inherent in the total (manual and automated) system, and control usage of the system to minimize some of the delays. If you attempt to monitor all aspects of the system and produce all possible reports, then, because of the amount of time required to use the system, there will probably be delays in the system that you simply cannot live with.

4. Choose a system that will help you to minimize

delays. Look for a system that will simplify the input process and that will allow you to select the kind of reports that you want. If you need fast entry of the data, will it be possible for more than one person to use the microcomputer at the same time? Will you be able to enter data into more than one computer, and then later combine all of the data for processing? Will the printer be fast enough to produce the reports? If you choose to print a large number of long reports, then, since your microcomputer will probably be tied up for all of the time that the printing is taking place, you will not be able to enter data during this time. Will this type of delay make use of the system difficult?

As you can tell, I have some rather severe reservations concerning the utility of such a system. My major recommendation is that you approach the use of such a system carefully. Treat the system as a tool to help you solve a problem, not as a solution to the problem. Plan what you are going to do, and decide in advance how you will handle the time and resource problems associated with the use of this type of system.

Data Retrieval

Every information system performs a number of functions, including the entry, storage, access, manipulation, and printing of data. The entry of data has been discussed previously in this section. The printing of data in the form of reports or in graphical form has also been discussed. The manipulation of the data takes several forms, including sorting, string manipulation, and numerical computations. The need for both numerical computations and string manipulations has been previously discussed. The two major purposes of sorting data are to arrange the data in order so that sequential access to data will be simplified and so that reports can be produced in the desired order.

The ability to access files both sequentially and directly is important since certain operations are facilitated by the type of access. When an information system is designed, it is not always possible to determine in advance all the ways that you might wish to access the data. Since you wish to create a private information system that is as flexible as possible, it will be necessary to design the files so that you will be able to choose either sequential or direct access, i.e., so that you will be able to access a file sequentially at one time and access the same file directly at another time. It is therefore imperative that your software development system allow you to do this.

When a file is accessed sequentially, you will be scanning forward or backward in the file, one record at a time. If the file has been sorted or arranged in a usable manner, then certain operations are facilitated. As an example, consider a report in which you will print information concerning all of the employees in your department, and the report is to be arranged in order by name. If you sort the employee data in order by name, then the processing is both simple and fast.

If you wish to print the same type of report, but only for one subdepartment, then a combination of direct and sequential access is useful. In this case a direct access to the first employee record in the subdepartment, followed by sequential access to all of the remaining employee records for the subdepartment, will produce the desired results. Direct access by itself is useful if you need to view the employee record for a single employee. The ability to access records directly in a file also provides the fundamental mechanism required to link together records that are logically associated, no matter what database or file management system you are using.

The retrieval of data is strongly related to the manner in which it is stored. The design of the file structure of your private information system is critical since it will determine whether data in the files can be linked together (and therefore made useful) and how long it will take to access the data. Consider the following:

You have a file that contains information about employees in your department. Each record in the file contains information concerning the employees and their skills, and individual records have the form given in Diagram 6.3, where the information for the skills possessed by each employee varies with the number of skills. If an employee has no special skills, there would be no *skill* fields in the record for that employee. If an employee has three skills, then there will be exactly three skill fields in the record for that employee. In general, if an employee has *n* skills, then there will be *n* skill fields in the employee record. This kind of record has all of the information for an employee all together in one place, so it is quite convenient to enter, store, manipulate, and report the data. Given the name of the employee, it is also possible quickly to find all of the skills associated with that employee. Assume that you have structured your data file in this manner because you have not anticipated the need to access the data in any other manner.

DIAGRAM 6.3

NAME	TEL NO	DATE HIRED	SALARY	SKILL 1	SKILL 2	.

Now you find that there is a need to find all of the employees with a particular skill. How can this be done? If the file is structured as shown in Diagram 6.3, you will need to examine each record in your data file (a sequential search) to find out which employees have the desired skill. If your file is large, this may be a time-consuming operation. If this procedure must be performed frequently, then a considerable amount of time must be devoted to it.

If we restructure the original data file, we might end up with two files that have the types of records depicted in Diagram 6.4.

Now we can find the names of employees possessing a certain skill in a much faster manner. We can sort the new skill records in order by skill. A direct access to the first *new skill record* with the desired skill will allow us to obtain the number of the first employee with this skill. A direct access to the *new employee file*, using the employee number just obtained, will allow us to get the name of the employee. We can perform a sequential scan of the new skill file from the point of the record in this file that was

DIAGRAM 6.4

New employee record

NAME	TEL NO	DATE HIRED	SALARY	EMPLOYEE NO

New skill record

EMPLOYEE NO	SKILL

obtained by the direct access, finding the number of each of the employees that possess the desired skill. As each employee number is obtained, it can be used to find the corresponding employee name in the new employee file. The sequential scan of the new skill file will stop as soon as we run out of records in that file that have the desired skill. If the percentage of employees with the desired skill is small (say, less than half of all employees), then this type of file structure will allow us to associate names with specific skills in an efficient manner. The original problem, associating skills with specific names, can still be solved using these files, but the amount of time for this process will now be greater.

When files are designed and the paths that link the files together are determined, it should first be done independently of the type of database or file management system that you expect to use. This will allow an implementation independent file structure and therefore facilitate a better understanding of the nature of the data itself. Once a database or file management system has been selected, the independent file structure design can then be converted into a design that is specific to the chosen database or file management system. This conversion is relatively easy to do and does not require extensive time.

After the file design has been converted to the specific system that you will use, it will usually have to be fine tuned. Minor modifications will then be made to the file structure in order to facilitate certain procedures and to speed up parts of the system. This three-step method of file structure creation has a number of advantages:

1. Since the original system is designed in an implementation independent manner, more of the nature of the data itself will be understood.
2. If you decide to change the database or file management system, the redesign effort will be minimal.
3. The effects of fine tuning your system will be localized. Thus, the scope of the changes due to fine tuning will be small, allowing easier debugging of the programs.
4. As you add, change, or delete programs, the effects upon the data files will be minimized.
5. As you add, change, or delete fields or record types, the effects upon the remainder of the data files will be minimal.

As you can see from this list, this approach to the development of a file structure will (usually) lead to a flexible system design. When changes are made to the file structure or to the programs (and such changes will be made), the effects of the changes will be minimized.

6.6 Integrated Packages

A number of software packages on the market will individually perform each of the tasks required by your development system. For example, you can purchase different software that can be used to: (1) write programs (an editor), (2) run programs and manage data, (3) draw graphs, or (4) communicate with other computers.

There are a number of high-quality software packages of each type available, with each package performing its assigned task correctly and (relatively) inexpensively. Unfortunately, when you wish to combine two or more of these functions, you may have some difficulties.

An editor, for example, is basically a word processing system used to write programs. Since the word processor has the capability of producing letters, documents, etc., it is natural to think of combining, for example, word processing and graphics. Unfortunately, the popular word processing systems usually do not have a graphics capability of their own. Even worse, graphs produced by graphics systems usually contain special control characters for the printer or the screen, and so they are totally incompatible with the word processing systems. This means that there is no way to insert graphs into the text documents produced by many of the popular word processors. This problem of incompatibility is not restricted just to word processing and graphics systems. You may occasionally find that you wish to combine functions that are performed well by individual software packages, but the software packages are themselves incompatible.

There is a movement in the industry toward multifunction software packages. For example, a package might combine word processing, graphics, database, spreadsheets, and communications. You must still be careful to determine that the multifunction software packages will allow you to combine the specific functions that you are interested in, but the probability of compatibility is higher with a multifunction package than it is with individual packages written by different organizations. Not only must the package be multifunction, but the individual functions must be integrated in such a manner as to allow the combinations of the functions that you desire.

There are other aspects of multifunction software packages that you will need to be careful about.

1. Multifunction software packages are usually much larger than one individual package, so you will need to make sure that you have enough disk space and enough main memory. The disk space problem can usually be solved by making sure that you purchase a hard disk machine. The main memory problem is usually solved by having at least 256K main memory, but you may use a multifunction package that requires even more. In order to overcome this problem, use a computer that will allow you easily to add more main memory. There are two common ways to add more main memory: the first is to

add more memory chips of the same type that is already being used, and the second is to add larger memory chips. In either case you will be limited both by the number of places where you may insert memory chips in the computer and by the operating system. Operating systems all have an upper bound on the total amount of main memory, and the main memory that you add may not exceed this upper bound.

2. The scope of each of the functions in a multifunction software package may be smaller than the scope of the function of corresponding individual packages. For example, an editor in a word processing package may allow you to copy a piece of a program from one location to another within the same file, but a multifunction software package may not provide this same service. As another example, an individual file management package may allow you rapid access to a given record in a file, but the file management function of a multifunction package may not provide this service.

3. Since multifunction software packages are more complex than individual software packages, they are more likely to contain errors, both errors in each function and errors in the interface between the functions. A general rule of thumb is: The more complex the software is, the higher the probability that it will contain errors.

Multifunction software packages offer both distinct advantages and disadvantages. The major advantage is the greater capability. The major disadvantages are derived from the complexity of the package, but the greater capability is the direct cause of the complexity. It thus follows that the disadvantages are a direct consequence of the major advantage, meaning that there is a trade-off. If you want the greater capability, then you must be willing to accept some of the disadvantages and try to minimize them.

One way to minimize the disadvantage of a reduced function is to use both individual software packages and multifunction packages together. For example:

Assume that you want to print both text and graphs in documents, so you purchase a multifunction software package that is advertised as having this capability. After using the system for a period of time, you discover that the word processing portion of the system does not have all of the functions that you would like it to have. You discover an individual word processing system that has all of the functions that you want; and you also discover that you can use the files created by this individual word processing system as if they were files created by the word processing function within the multifunction system (the text files created by this individual word processing system are compatible with the word processing function in your multifunction system). You can, in this case, use the individual word processing system to create the text, use the multifunction system to produce the graphs, and then use the multifunction system to combine both the text and the graphs in printed reports.

It is clear that the above solution has the disadvantage of additional cost, but each one of the desired functions is provided by the total system (the individual system and the multifunction system working together).

Multifunction systems are relatively new on the market, so you should expect that there will be some problems with them. But remember, increased capabilities, especially if you really need them, are often worth a little more money.

A multifunction software development system (like Ashton-Tate's FRAMEWORK) may save you money or may simplify the process of integrating the various parts of your system.

6.7 Selection of a Software Development System

Discuss the choice of the software development system with your software technician before the implementation of the system starts. I assume here that you will already have a microcomputer system or that you plan to get one in the immediate future. Most software packages for the construction of a private information system can be used on a wide variety of microcomputers, but new system software might work on only one kind of computer (the IBM compatible computers). If you don't have an IBM compatible, it might take a considerable amount of time for a new package to be available for your particular computer.

You will probably need more than one system development package. You will need a word processor to create your programs, and you will need at least one database or file management system. In addition, there may not be a single software development system on the market that will do all of the things that you want done. You may need to use two or more of them together to achieve the desired effect.

Some of the more popular software development systems are: (1) dBASE II, dBASE III, and FRAMEWORK from Ashton-Tate and (2) 1–2–3 and Symphony from Lotus. I have built a number of systems using both dBASE II and dBASE III, and I believe that dBASE III would do most of the things that you need done; but, I am not specifically recommending this package for your applications. You and your software technician must make your own decisions, based upon the evaluations of your information needs. New software development systems are appearing all the time, and just the one that you need may soon be available. But, if you wait too long, you will lose a number of opportunities for success. Choose a software development system that will do most of the things that you want to do. It is usually not necessary to choose a system that will do all of the things that you ever wanted to do. Select a software system that: (1) runs on your microcomputer, (2) has a reputation for reliability, (3) provides you with a query capability, (4) provides you with most of the basic features that you want, (5) can interface with other software systems (if necessary), (6) is reasonably fast, and (7) is easy to program and to use.

The selection of a software development system may

have to be left to your software technician, but do not select a software development system just because the software technician has used it before. Select one because it is the best one for the job. A good software technician will be able to learn how to use a new software development system in a reasonably small amount of time.

You might need more than one software development system to create a private information system that will perform all of the functions that you want done. In many cases, it is possible to integrate different systems in a useful manner. Systems like FRAMEWORK allow an added dimension of flexibility since they allow you both stand-alone capability and to integrate database, word processing, spreadsheets, and graphics. For example, you could use:

1. dBASE III for your heavy database processing,
2. WordStar for word processing,
3. FRAMEWORK or Lotus 1-2-3 for spreadsheets,
4. FRAMEWORK for graphics, and
5. FRAMEWORK for the integration of database processing, word processing, spreadsheets, and graphics.

CHAPTER 7

The New Information System: Part I

7.1 Using the Formal Information System for Ordinary Tasks

The organization's information system contains records of a number of different types of transactions. If you can gain direct access to this information, you will be able to use it to do your job better. Access to the data involves each of the following: (1) permission to access the data files, (2) a terminal to access the computer itself, and (3) specialized hardware and software to help you communicate with the organization's computer.

If the data in your organization is "owned" by individual departments, you will probably have a great deal of difficulty gaining access to data not specifically owned by your own department. This is because each individual department usually is jealous of its own prerogatives. Any data that is owned by a department other than your own is extraordinarily difficult to gain access to. The department that owns the data will have several concerns, including:

1. The information is sensitive and you should not even see it.
2. You should not be able to change any of the data.
3. You have not proven that you even need to see the

data. This may cause trouble for you because you probably do not wish to make known your intentions to create a private information system.

If the data is treated as an organizational resource, i.e., if the data is not owned by any person or department in the organization (the enlightened approach), then it may be easier to gain access to the data. In this case, you will need to obtain permission from the database administrator or the person in charge of the data files. In any event, you will still need permission from someone to gain access. It is important to be able to access the data directly, rather than indirectly through reports, since you will often need to use the data stored in the computer (actually on the disks) in a manner that is different from the way in which others use it.

You will need to obtain direct access to the data files in your organization's information system.

If data is not treated as an organizational resource, you may have difficulty obtaining permission to access it.

The organizational information system has been designed to provide information in a rather rigid form. Someone else has decided for you what information you will need to do your job. In addition, the reports that you get may actually have been designed for people doing another job, with copies sent to you because the information in the reports might be related to your job. Examine all of the reports that you receive on a regular basis. Chances are good that at least 25 percent of all the reports that you receive are really designed for someone doing a different job. In any event, the standard information that you receive from the information system will seldom allow you to be creative and to perform your job in a superior manner. In addition, the standard reports simply cannot satisfy the information needs in a changing environment. It is not unusual for reports to be two years behind significant changes in the environment. If your job has changed in a significant manner, about two years will elapse before the information system catches up with the changes.

The reports that you receive from the organization's information system are rigid in nature. They seldom provide the kind of information that will allow you to demonstrate initiative and to be creative.

In most modern information systems, there are two kinds of data files: those that can be accessed directly through the operating system and those that cannot. To access a data file through the operating system, use an operating system function. For example, on some computers you enter an operating system command like TYPE FILEA to display the entire contents of the data file with the name FILEA, one line at a time on the screen of your terminal. If your organization's information system uses a database management system or a sophisticated file management system, then you will probably not be able to access the data files directly. It will be necessary for you to use the database management system itself or a query facility to access the data files. If you are not a programmer, then you will only be able to use the query facility. Some types of query facilities are easy to use, and some are quite difficult. Nevertheless, most query facilities require only a knowledge of the query facility itself and an understanding of how the data is organized (stored). A knowledge of programming is seldom required to operate a query facility. If your information system has a query facility, then you should be able to use it from your own terminal or from a microcomputer with the correct communication software and hardware.

> If you cannot access the data files directly through the operating system and if you are not a programmer, then you will need to use a query facility.

One way in which you might use the data stored in the organization's information system is to scan through the data, perform your own manipulations, and create your own reports. Your organization will probably bar you from making any changes to their data files, but you may usually access the files if you do not make any changes. Since query facilities usually have a rudimentary reporting capability, you will be able to perform each of the following functions without programming:

1. Browse through the data, looking for anything of interest. This includes, but is not limited to: trends, inconsistencies, incorrect values, missing records, and missing data. Once you understand what should be contained in the data files, browsing through them often allows you to spot problems that you might not find in any other way.

2. Produce your own reports. The reports that you produce will be for your own private use. The reports might be quite simple in nature or they might be rather complex. The reporting capability of a query system allows you to select records with a complex selection criteria, to perform both arithmetic and text manipulations, and to format the result into a professional-looking report. This will allow you to overcome most if not all of the problems that you encounter trying to use reports that are not really designed with you in mind. You may delete unnecessary data, include additional data, perform calculations that you now have to do yourself, and you can print the report in the format that you personally prefer. A good query facility allows you to build your own private information system within the organization's information system.

> You can use the organization's existing information system
> in novel and creative ways, if you have access to the data
> itself. A query facility is often required for this purpose.

It is also possible to pass (or copy) selected data from
the organization's data files to your own microcomputer.
If you have a database or file management system on
your microcomputer, then you can perform each of the
two functions listed above on your own computer. Being
able to perform these functions on your own computer
has several advantages. The primary ones are:

1. Once the data has been transferred to your microcomputer, then you can put the data into your own files
and use your own query facility. Your own query facility
will probably be easier to use than the organization's
query facility. Remember that the software on a microcomputer is often much easier to use than the software
on a larger computer.

2. When you use your own computer to perform extra
processing of the data, you do not have to account for or
pay for the processing time. When you use a large computer, you will be billed for all of the resources that you
use. When you use your own microcomputer, you pay
nothing beyond the original purchase price and periodic
maintenance.

3. Since you now have your own copy of the data, you
can make whatever changes you wish to.

> If you can select data from the organization's information
> system and pass it to your microcomputer, then you will
> have an easy-to-use and cost effective alternative to using
> the organization's large computer.

The cost of a microcomputer system (computer, printer,
and modem) and the associated software will probably be

less than £7,000. This figure is small enough that most organizations will allow you as a middle manager to purchase such a system from company funds. If the expenditure is not allowed, then the cost is still low enough that you can probably afford it from your personal funds. Although £7,000 is not a small amount of money for the middle manager to spend for a computer system to be used in a private information system, it is still less than a good automobile and may make advancement to higher-level management possible. If you have to purchase your own computer system, consider it an investment in your future. In many circumstances you may also be able to take a tax credit for the investment.

The cost of a microcomputer system is small enough that many organizations will allow you to purchase one using normal operating funds.

7.2 Using the Private Information System

The formal information system, i.e., the organization's information system, may not have been designed to collect some of the information that you personally need. In this case, the specific information that you need will not be available from the organizational information system, and you will have to gather the information yourself. The primary uses of a private information system are to obtain and process data or to perform processes not available through the organization's information system.

Use your private information system to help you perform the tasks that you cannot perform using the organization's information system or that would be too expensive to perform using the organization's information system.

If you are not allowed access to the data stored in the organization's information system, then you will need to do everything with your own private information system. In particular, you will need to gather and enter all of the relevant information yourself, or you will need to assign someone in your department to perform this task.

7.3 More Free Time

The first major use of both the organization's information and your private information system is to save you time. You have two precious resources: time and energy. You probably cannot increase the amount of energy that you have, but you can use your time more wisely, and you can reduce the demands on your energy.

Since you probably run out of energy before you run out of time, it is important that you schedule your activities. Remember that you want to work smart, not hard. This means that you should not work more than an 8-hour day and not more than a 40-hour week, unless there is a real emergency. If you find that you regularly work more than 40 hours a week, a major revision of your work schedule and a major reevaluation of your definition of an emergency are necessary. If you work too much, you will not be able to work either productively or creatively. Create a balance between your job activities on the one hand and your social, home, and family activities on the other hand. If you invest time wisely in your social, home, and family activities, you will have more energy to spend on your job, and the time spent at work will be more productive. Schedule your personal activities so that they will contribute to your overall plan for success.

Have a reasonable balance between work and nonwork activities. The correct balance will help you to spend your work time more productively.

Start your schedule with an evaluation of your current work. Map out your week on a day-by-day basis. Determine how much time you spend on each task and examine each task to determine its nature. Any task that can reasonably be delegated to a subordinate must be delegated. If you try to do everything yourself, you will have neither the time nor the energy to be creative and innovative. Delegation will also allow you to make good use of the talents, abilities, and ideas of others. It will also allow others to develop their creative abilities.

> Delegate any tasks that you do not absolutely have to do yourself.

When you examine your weekly work schedule, you will probably find that there are a number of tasks that can be delegated to others. You will probably also find some tasks that are repetitive in nature, but, for reasons of your own, you prefer to perform these tasks yourself. Be careful on the delegation of tasks to subordinates. Some of the tasks that have been assigned to you are critical in nature. Your job performance may be evaluated on the success or failure of these critical tasks. Try to delegate the time-consuming part of these critical tasks to others, but remember that you are ultimately responsible for the success or failure of these tasks. Make sure that you monitor the performance of these critical tasks on a regular basis. You may wish to use your private information system to assist in monitoring the performance of these critical tasks, if you cannot receive the requisite information from the organization's information system.

> Identify the tasks that are critical to your job. Make sure that you monitor them on a regular basis.

Examine the tasks that you have reserved for yourself. If any of these tasks require a large amount of time or if they are repetitive in nature, you might wish to use either the organization's or your private information system to help you reduce the time invested in each of these tasks. Before you can use an information system to help you reduce the time involved in the performance of a task, you must first understand all of the aspects of the task itself. Examine each of these tasks and account for each decision and action necessary to perform each task. Enumerate the kind of data that is necessary for each task and write a detailed description of how each task is performed.

> Write a detailed description of each task that is either repetitive in nature or requires a considerable amount of time. Also list all of the data required by each task.

Once you have a detailed description of each of these tasks, and you have listed the data required for each task, then you can use the services of a software technician. It is important that you understand each of the tasks yourself, before you try to automate any part of them. You must formulate goals for your personal success, and the choice of procedures to be automated should directly contribute to this plan. You are the person in charge of the development of the private information system, not the software technician. The main task of the software technician is to implement what you want done. If you don't know what you want done, the software technician will not be able to provide you with a good private information system.

7.4 System Development

When you build an information system for yourself, either an extension of the organization's information system or your private information system, you must build it so that it can evolve and change over a period of time. Your private information system must not be constructed in such a way that changes cannot be made without a complete redesign of the system. This is one of the areas where the choice of a good software technician is important. The better your choice of a software technician, the lower the probability that any major redesign efforts will need to be done.

You will find that your understanding of your information needs will evolve over a period of time.

One of the important tasks of your software technician is to design and construct an information system that is flexible. It must not be either time consuming nor expensive to make changes to your system. You, not the software technician, must take the primary responsibility for the overall design of the private information system since you know your job better than the technician does. This is an important point: You are the one who knows what must be done—the software technician (usually) doesn't. The software technician's major contribution will be to implement your ideas in an efficient manner. Don't rely on the software technician for too many ideas. Your own subordinates will have many more good ideas on improvements than the software technician will.

I recommend that you perform each of the following:

1. Make a survey of how you spend your time at work.
2. Determine how much time you spend on each task.
3. Delegate to subordinates the tasks that you should not do and the tasks that you do not absolutely have to do yourself.
4. Examine the tasks that you have reserved for yourself.
5. Write a definitive description of each of the tasks enumerated in item 4, and list the data required

for each task. Specify where you get each data
item.

6. Use the skills of a software technician to help you
   design, on a logical level, as complete an information system as you can. Remember that the purpose of the information system is to save you time
   and energy. Don't be so ambitious that your job
   with the private information system takes more of
   your time than your job does without the private
   information system. This warning is more important than you might think. Most first-time computer users are too ambitious. They simply try to
   automate *everything*, rather than be selective, and
   they end up spending more time than they should.

The software technician will then take your overall design and transform it into one suitable for implementation on a microcomputer. The organization's information
system will allow you to browse and search through organizational data. You may even be able to use the organization's information system to produce a number of reports for your own purposes; but, in the end, your major
tool will still be the private information system on your
microcomputer.

You must take the responsibility for the development of
your private information system. You must make sure
that you understand just what you want before any construction of the information system starts.

The software technician will build an information system
from your detailed specifications.

Your specifications will first be transformed into an
overall system design. The requisite data files and

programs will be determined by the software technician. Since the entire information system cannot be built all at once, it will be necessary to assign approximate times for the completion of each part of the information system. It is very difficult to estimate just how long it will take to complete each part of the information system. This is one of the places where the choice of a good software technician is critical: a poor or mediocre technician will take much longer to complete a system than a good one will. If your choice of a software technician is bad enough, the information system will never be done. I know of a situation where a large restaurant hired a youngster just out of high school to build an information system for them. After a year and a half of fruitless labour, the project was abandoned and the computer was sold. The restaurant never did come to understand that an amateur is not capable of building a quality information system.

Once the system has been designed, you will have to determine the order in which the parts of the system will be completed. Some parts of the system may be so strongly related to each other that you cannot have one part without certain others. By the time that your system is (basically) completed, you will find that some changes to the system will be necessary. The reasons for the changes include:

1. You have changed your mind about what the system should do or the manner in which certain parts of the system should operate (your understanding has evolved).
2. There has been a communication problem between you and the software technician. You thought that you were saying one thing, and the technician thought that you were saying something else.
3. You have decided to add new functions to the system.
4. Parts of the system are too difficult or time consuming to use.
5. Parts of the system must be speeded up.

You will need to decide which parts of the information system will be implemented first. Use the judgment of the software technician to help create an implementation schedule.

Assume that there will be some problems with the implementation schedule. Also assume that a number of changes will have to be made to the new information system before it will satisfy you.

7.5 Using Your Free Time

The first task of reorganizing your job is to reduce the total amount of time that you spend doing it. This will allow you the free time that you need to be creative and innovative. You may then be able to apply your creative talents to further reducing the demands on your time and on the time of those who work for you. The real recognition for your creative efforts will come when you can provide a valuable service to your superiors that has not been provided previously or by substantially reducing operating costs. You must make sure that the reduction in operating costs is not accompanied by a decrease in certain critical operating variables (like quality). The real rewards come when you can demonstrate that you have a better way to do things, not merely a different way.

Aim for a substantial reduction of demands on your time. Use the new free time to develop new procedures for your department. Provide your superiors with a service that they need but which they currently do not have. Reduce your department's operating costs and/or substantially increase its profits. Develop better ways of doing things.

7.6 Using the Formal and Private Information Systems Together

Your understanding of the problems that you wish to solve will evolve over a period of time. You may wish to transfer selected data from the organization's information system to your microcomputer so that you can perform experiments with it. Once you have determined that certain operations with the data are useful to you, you might wish to perform these operations on the organization's information system, if you are allowed to. You might choose to perform the operations on your organization's computer either because it is easier to perform them there or because the right facilities (such as statistical packages) are there. Similarly, after an evaluation you might decide that some of the operations that you currently perform on the organization's computer might best be performed using your own microcomputer.

Be flexible in your thinking. Think of your enhancements to the organization's information system (as offered through its query facility) and all of the functions performed for you on your own microcomputer as being part of your total, private information system. Review your information system on a regular basis. Don't allow it to solidify into an inflexible system. As you gain experience with your own information system, make the necessary adjustments, including the movement of procedures and data from one machine to another, if it will improve overall performance. Solicit suggestions for the improvement of your private information system from all those who work with it. You will find that a wealth of ideas are available from the users, if you encourage them to present their ideas. Many people get ideas faster when they have an opportunity to see something in action. Thus, after your private information system is operating, you may be able to get a number of good ideas from the users of the system, where these same people might have had few good ideas before the system started to operate.

CHAPTER 8

The New Information System: Part II

8.1 Plan a New Approach

After you have delegated some of your current responsibilities and have automated some others, you should have enough free time to do some research. Your main goal is to provide higher-level management with a service that they need but cannot currently get or to substantially reduce the operating costs of your department. If you choose to reduce the operating costs of your department, you must do so in a manner that will not antagonize your subordinates. For example, you must not lay them off during lean times, and you must not make them work longer hours than they normally do. I once worked for an organization that started losing money during a downswing in the economy. A new manager of one of the manufacturing departments required that all of the members of his department take an enforced two-week vacation. If an employee had accrued vacation time, he or she had to use it, otherwise the employee was laid off for two weeks. I started looking for another job right away.

> Plan your approach so that you do not antagonize those who work for you.

Your first step is to understand the goals of your department and to understand how each person in your department contributes to these goals. Conduct a survey to determine how each person (or category of worker) performs his or her job. Ask each individual for suggestions on how his or her job can be done more efficiently.

> Determine the goals and patterns of work in your organization.

Once you have an overall understanding of the work done in your department, use your software technician to help you determine how information flows into, out of, and within your department, and compare this information with the best of the suggestions from your workers. Your software technician should be an expert in this area. Evaluate the flow of information for areas where obvious improvements should be made, map out a new information flow, specify new work procedures, and then present the planned improvements to the people affected by them. The reasons for presenting the proposed improvements to your workers are:

1. You wish to establish a good psychological atmosphere for change. You want the workers to feel that they are helping to make their own jobs easier and more productive.
2. You want to verify that the proposed changes are reasonable and will really work. The people that actually do the work are in a good position to evaluate your plans for strengths and weaknesses.

> Determine the flow of information within your department. Revise the flow of information and work procedures to improve the departmental operations.

> Present the changes to the people who are affected by
> them. Use their suggestions to modify the proposed
> changes as necessary.

Restructuring the information flow allows you to make
improvements in several areas:

1. Individual operations within the department can
   be performed more efficiently.
2. Overall performance of the department can be
   increased.
3. An evaluation of the kind of data available within
   the department can be performed. From the evaluation, you will be able to determine what data is
   collected but never used, what data is needed but
   not available, and potential, additional uses for
   the data.

I recommend that you make changes in the information flow in your department so that:

1. Successes and failures will be easy to evaluate.
2. The time invested by your workers under the new
   information flow is not greater than the time required by the old information flow.
3. All changes are performed manually, rather than
   by a computer. After you have verified that a new
   technique is successful, you may then automate it.

You must be able to verify to your superiors that your
changes have caused an improvement. In order to do this,
you will need to determine how you will measure and
evaluate both the new techniques and the old ones. Also
determine the basis for comparisons of the techniques.

8.2 Work out the Details of the Goals

The implementation of your plans should get you closer
to specific goals, so make sure that your goals have been

specified before you try to implement any plans. For example, the goal of greater efficiency for the entire department is just too broad. From your evaluation of the work patterns and information flows within your department, you might determine that a large percentage of labour goes into the performance of a specific task. This is a good candidate for improvement since a considerable improvement in performance is possible. Target this specific task for improvement, rather than a general one.

Be specific about the goals that you wish to achieve. The more specific the goals, the easier they will be to achieve.

When you start to make plans to achieve your goals, consider those functions that take a large number of worker hours. Such functions are often good candidates for savings.

A few years ago I worked for a major manufacturer of integrated circuits. The organization had several manufacturing plants, and each type of circuit was manufactured at a number of different plants. A number of variables could affect the percentage of working circuits (the yield). The variables included the characteristics of the materials and chemicals used, the precision of the machinery, and the correct use of the machinery. Test circuits were produced right along with regular production circuits, using the same machinery and materials, but with different machine settings. Both the regular production circuits and the test circuits were then evaluated for operating characteristics. The manager of manufacturing could then evaluate variations in the manufacturing process to see if the yield could be increased through variation of machine settings. The evaluation information was then analyzed to determine which factors in the manufacturing process had the greatest effect upon the yield. Since the interrelationship between the factors was quite complex, it was necessary to use a computer to manipulate the various factors. I wrote a program that would allow the manufacturing engineers to search for complex relationships between the factors in an attempt to determine which manufacturing characteristics would lead to which kind of finished product performance problems. The potential advantages of this project were:

1. Increased yields for a number of different types of integrated circuits within the original department.
2. A considerable savings in the amount of time that engineers needed to evaluate the effect of manufacturing changes on the quality of the finished product.
3. Information that would increase the yields at all other manufacturing plants.

The successful completion of the project would make this middle manager visible within the organization both for the reduced operational costs within his own department and for the new information that would lead to increased yields in every manufacturing plant.

Sometimes the areas that you should investigate are the most obvious, coming directly from the major, assigned task of your department.

The importance of an improvement might be measured in more than one way. It might reduce your operating expenses, increase your production capacity, and might help other departments performing the same function.

You must be specific about what you wish to achieve. You must have concrete goals (like the determination of which manufacturing characteristics lead to which performance characteristics) and a specific plan to achieve these goals.

As another example of concrete goals, I present the following:

While working for a software house, I was responsible for the development of a complete purchasing system for a major foreign oil producer. The purchasing department was responsible for the purchase of over $1 billion of materials each year. They felt that the (outdated) techniques being used were responsible for the loss of over $100 million per year. Their specific goals were to improve performance in each of the following areas: selection of potential vendors, bids, awarding of the purchase orders, shipment of materials to requesters, and the payment of vendors.

Both high- and middle-level managers were selected to attend seminars at major American universities to learn the latest concepts in purchasing. After the managers had completed the seminars, an evaluation of several problem areas was conducted by the purchasing department. A major accounting firm was then engaged to assist in an evaluation of the purchasing department information flow, and the firm made recommendations for its improvement. The management of purchasing, using the information gained at the seminars and the help of the analysts from the major accounting firm, designed a new purchasing system. The specific goals of this new system were:

1. To base the selection of potential vendors on quantifiable measurements such as past performance, if the vendors had previously supplied equipment.
2. To employ a selection technique that would allow the use of both old and new suppliers, with a reasonable balance between old and new suppliers.
3. To control the bidding process so that bids were received only from authorized bidders.
4. To award purchase orders on a rational, objective basis.
5. To inspect all shipments received from vendors, to record the receipt of a shipment at a warehouse, to record the storage location of each item in the warehouse, and to forward shipments to requesters according to a schedule.
6. To pay a vendor's invoice only when all of the pur-

chase order items have been received and when the vendor has met all of the requirements of the purchase order.

7. To pay only the amounts agreed to in the original purchase order or in additions to the original purchase order.

The original goal of saving money led to the evaluation of the information flow and the processing techniques. A determination of the major problem areas was then made, and specific goals for each of these problem areas were established. A new manual information flow was designed, and new techniques were established for the processing of information in each of the previously identified problem areas. After the manual flows and processes were evaluated and corrected, the selection of a software house (the equivalent of your software technician) was made to automate portions of the entire process.

The more thought and planning that you give to your private information system before you use the services of a software technician, the higher the probability of the success of the system.

8.3 Using the Software Technician

You are in charge of the efforts to create a private information system, and you should learn to use the skills of your software technician in an effective manner. Do not give vague directions to your technician with the hope that he or she will accomplish a miracle. You must determine the goals of your system, and you must make the plans to achieve these goals. The software technician can help you with suggestions, with some guidance, and with the application of his or her specific skills, but you, not the technician, are the problem solver. The software technician is there only to help you create your private information system.

> You must take the overall responsibility for the private information system. The software technician can help you implement your ideas, but you, not the technician, must originate the ideas and solve the problems.

When you use the skills of a software technician, you must be able to evaluate the recommendations of the technician. You must be able to determine when a recommendation will save you time, save you money, and lead to a flexible system, or when a recommendation will merely make the system easier for the technician to build. Thus, you must determine when a recommendation is made for your benefit and when it is made for the technician's benefit.

Use the technician's skills to complement your own. You understand more about your department and your goals than does the technician, so it is not reasonable for the software technician to be the project manager. You can use the software technician at each stage of the development of your private information system. For example:

1. You plan a schedule for the interviewing of your workers and have the software technician either carry out the actual interview or assist in the interview process.
2. Have the technician prepare information flow diagrams for you so that you can see how information flows into, out of, and through your department.
3. You analyze the information flow diagram(s) and determine the areas where improvements should be made. Work with the technician to determine the nature of the improvements. You specify the nature of the improvements and let the technician recommend alternative (one or more) methods for implementation of the improvements. Then you review the technician's recommendations and select the ones that you like best.

> Complement your own skills with those of the software technician.

8.4 Program the New Algorithms

It is tempting to let the software technician write all of the programs. After all, that is one of the things the technician is good at and you probably are not. Unfortunately, if you leave the programs entirely up to the technician, you will ultimately lose control of the project. If you do not somehow take an active part in writing the programs, the technician will make a number of choices in the design of the algorithms that you should be making.

It is not expected that you will actually program but that you will participate in a meaningful way in the programming effort. I recommend that you accomplish this by writing the specifications for each program. You must determine, for each major function, what the goals of the private information system are and how each of the goals will be accomplished. You must specify, in a logical sense, how each part of your system will work. Remember that each program is merely a set of instructions in a language that the computer can understand. You must determine what these instructions should be, and the software technician will translate your instructions into the correct computer language. You don't want the software technician to design the system for you; you want to design the system yourself and have the technician implement it for you.

> You must write the specifications for each of the major functions of the system. The software technician will then translate these specifications into programs for you. If you let the technician write the specifications, then you will ultimately lose control of the project.

The logical design of a private information system is not as difficult as you might think. You first specify the goals to be achieved by your system, then you specify the major functional parts of the system that will allow you to achieve these goals. Then you specify how the functions will be carried out. Once you have instructed the software technician in each of these areas, the technician will then implement your design. The implementation will consist of a file structure, programs, formats for inputs, and formats for outputs. You and the actual users of the system (you and/or some of your workers) should review each of the system parts for the following characteristics: (1) comprehensiveness, (2) correctness, (3) ease of use, (4) speed, (5) clarity, and (6) flexibility. Item 5 requires that instructions for the use of the system be clear, concise, and easy to follow.

In addition, you must regularly review your information system to determine if it is actually getting you closer to your stated goals. You must also review your goals on a periodic basis. As you achieve certain goals, you might wish, for example, to add new ones or to modify existing ones.

Review the effectiveness of your private information system on a regular basis. Determine if you are achieving the goals for which your information system was designed.

8.5 Implement Your New System

As your private information system is being implemented, parts of the system will become available for use. Place selected parts of the system in operation first. Do not attempt to place the entire system in operation all at once. Evaluate selected parts of the system and make modifications as necessary. As each part of the system is placed in operation, fit it into the framework of the entire private information system. This type of testing is called *top-down testing*.

Plan to test your private information system in a top-down fashion. Start with the main module of the system and gradually add the remainder of the system.

If the system does not perform as expected, then one or more of the following contribute to the problem:

1. The original design of the system is faulty.

Your own concepts were incorrect. Don't be afraid of failure or of looking bad to the technician. You should expect that there will be some problems with your original design. After all, understanding is an evolutionary process.

2. The technician's implementation of your design is faulty (either an actual error or a communication problem).

When the project starts, the technician does not understand your problems as well as you do. The technician must also go through several phases of understanding. The technician's understanding will also evolve over a period of time. It is also possible that some of the programs (algorithms) are just plain wrong.

3. The system is being used in a manner other than what was intended (this is a common problem).

There may be a communication problem, where the technician thought that instructions for the use of the system were clear. Changes in the system may also account for instructions for the use of the system not matching the current version of the system.

4. The system is performing correctly, but the results are different from what you expected.

Your new system may be operating correctly, but when you compared it with information obtained from another source, the other information was incorrect. It is also possible that the form of the output is not what you expected, causing you to think that it is wrong, when it actually is correct. For example, in some systems, the number 1.2 might be printed by the computer as .12E1, a

form of scientific notation, causing you to think at first
glance that the output is incorrect.

Test your system with carefully selected data. The data
should be chosen so as to facilitate both quick and accurate testing of the system.

You must take the primary responsibility to determine
if the system is functioning properly, and the software
technician must take the responsibility for tracking
down the nature of the problem. In the case of a system
design error, you must make changes in the design. In
the case of an implementation error, the technician must
take the responsibility for correcting it.

You, not the software technician, must take the primary
responsibility for the testing of the system.

8.6 Review and Fine Tune Your System

While your private information system is being placed in
operation, the users will discover parts of the system that
should be made easier to use or that need to be made
faster. Both of these problems are so common that both
you and the technician should expect them to occur. Review the system on a regular basis both during and after
implementation. When possible, have the technician
take the appropriate corrective action. In some cases,
changes that appear to be relatively simple will involve
major changes in the system. With each major change of
the system, the technical aspects of the system become
harder to understand (for both you and the technician).
You should therefore discuss any changes with the technician to determine their effect. If the changes are minor,
go ahead and make them. If the changes are major, you
must determine if the changes should be made. Avoid

cosmetic changes since the total number of changes to the system increases the possibility of error. Cosmetic changes are those that do not need to be made either for the correct functioning of the system or for the ease of use of the system. They would be made strictly to improve the appearance of the operation.

You will need to examine your private information system for speed and ease of use, while parts of it are being installed and after it has become operational.

Fine tuning is making minor changes in the system so that it more nearly approximates the desired system. Do not expect your system to be perfect. You will probably start with an approximation of the system that you want, and then, as your understanding of the problems grows and as your familiarity with the system increases, corrections can be made. You will eventually reach the point where the system does almost everything that you want it to. Be careful about overdoing the fine tuning. Once the system has been 95 percent completed, for example, it make take 50 percent more work to make another 1 percent improvement.

Avoid making numerous and frivolous changes to the system. The more changes that you make, the less stable the system becomes.

8.7 Document the Improvements Obtained through the Use of Your Information System

As you use your private information system to create more free time, you will start to make improvements in your department. It is absolutely vital that you document the improvements. Record the values of the important parameters of your department before you make any changes. After you effect any changes, record the new parameter values. Since your changes must not lower the values of any of the critical success factors of your position, constantly monitor them to verify that they are nondecreasing. Record the specific techniques that lead to your successes, the amount of time required to effect the changes, the amount of money invested, the date the changes were put into effect, and the dates that you recorded the increases. Verify also that the changes are not just temporary and that they do not depend upon the times that the measurements were taken.

You should also record your failures. When you present your proposals to higher management, you will probably be asked to verify your findings. You can trace the evolution of your successes and answer unanticipated questions if you have information on both your successes and failures. The "have you considered the following..." and "what if you did..." questions often require you to be aware of both the successes and failures.

Be prepared to justify your results. To do this you will need to record all of the important aspects of your work.

CHAPTER 9

Creative Approaches

9.1 Creativity

Creative information system usage is the product of a flexible problem solving approach and of persistence. You must be a good problem solver, you must be willing to try to solve problems differently than others do, and you must stick to your plan until the problem is solved. Flexibility is a critical ingredient of creativity. If you attempt to solve your problems by extending the common approach, then you will often find yourself at a dead end. If you try to use a new approach to problem solving just to see what will happen, i.e., there is no reasonable basis for expecting that you will succeed, then you will probably waste your time and resources. Balance your creative efforts with a reasonable expectation of success.

I recommend that you do each of the following:

1. Examine the way that your department does business and determine how each worker supports the department's efforts. Do not be too concerned about the efficiency of each individual worker, but concentrate your efforts to understand your department as a system.

2. Look for obvious ways tó improve the flow of information within your department and to improve individual work techniques. Again, you should try to improve the entire department as a system, not individual work habits.

3. In your search for improvement, examine those information flows and work procedures that are in the mainstream of your department. Pay particular attention to those efforts that consume a large percentage of workhours and those that are directly related to the critical factors in your evaluation as a manager. You must make sure that you improve the statistics upon which you are evaluated as a manager as well as raising the overall performance of your department or providing new services to your superiors.

4. Always make your workers a part of the improvement effort. Find meaningful ways to reward their efforts to improve the departmental system. You absolutely must not give the impression that you are using your workers only to get ahead. Honestly help others to get ahead, and you will be more successful in your own efforts. Provide the opportunity for your workers to be creative and innovative. This will undoubtedly improve individual performance, and it will give you the opportunity to get some fresh ideas.

5. Examine each time-consuming or critical task in your department. Solicit suggestions about them from workers in your department. Answer the questions:

A. What is the problem that we are trying to solve through this worker's efforts?
B. How close do we come to solving the problem?
C. Why do we do it that way?
D. Is there a better way to do it?
E. Are there any other things that we can do?

6. Select a specific set (possibly only one) of problems to attack. Pick problems that have a reasonable chance of success and that will, if successfully completed, significantly advance your image in the organization. If you become involved in trying to solve too many problems all at the same time, then you probably will not be able to do a good job on any of them. If the problems that you attack are too hard, you will certainly waste a considerable amount of time and energy.

7. Devise a plan for solving the problem(s). In many

cases, you will find that your private information system will provide the key to success. The reason is simple: many problems are unsolved not because they are logically too hard to solve, but because people have not yet applied the right tools to solve them. Use not only the information system itself but also the information system techniques. An information flow diagram may immediately reveal a hidden problem and, in some cases, may even indicate a good solution.

8. Carefully tailor your private information system to help you solve the problems that you have selected to work on. Don't be too general—don't attempt to do everything with the information system. Determine the information that you need and tailor your private information system to provide you precisely with that information.

9. Get feedback from your workers and from your private information system on the success or failure of your projects. As your understanding of the problems grows, fine tune the information flow, the work procedures, and your private information system.

10. Remember to document each step of the project.

11. Don't be afraid to start all over again. You may select a problem to work on that looks good in the beginning but, for some reason, you can't finish it. The problem may be too hard to solve, or it may require more resources than you have. If a reasonable part of the original problem is still solvable, solve the part that you can handle. If the entire problem is too hard, look for another one. If you have some trouble with your first choice of a problem, don't give up. Persistence always pays off.

As a manager, you do not have time to do everything yourself. Your innovative approaches do not all have to be your own ideas. Get ideas from your workers, too. When you solicit ideas, take both a micro and a macro approach. Look for ideas to improve individual jobs and for ideas that will improve the entire department. Reserve judgment on ideas until you really understand them. Some bad ideas sound good when you first hear them but lose their appeal when you look at them closely. Some very good ideas sound ridiculous when you first hear them. One nice thing about a really good idea: the more you think about it, the more sense it makes.

In the following sections, we will look at some situations where innovative ideas have been applied. These situations are not designed to specifically tell you what to do in your position. They are designed to help you understand what creativity is and how to apply it. Individual situations call for different approaches. No two situations call for the same approach. Even two people faced with the same problems would try to solve their problems differently. You are not trying to learn specific techniques; rather, you are trying to get a feel for general approaches. As you examine each of the following situations, compare them with your own job. For each situation, ask yourself the questions: (1) In what way is this situation the same as mine? In what way is it different? (2) What creative approaches have been used? (3) Can I use the approaches directly in my own job? (4) Can I generalize the approach? (5) Can I use part of the approach? (6) Does either the problem or the approach to the solution ring a bell in my mind? (7) What specific things can I learn from these situations?

After you are done with these situations, if you still don't have any good ideas, examine some situations that you are familiar with. Ask the same questions about these situations.

9.2 The Sales Manager

You are the manager of a number of salespeople, and you wish to increase sales. You examine the features that make other sales organizations successful as a guideline to determine how you might improve your own sales group. An examination of your own sales group, conferences with your salespeople, and a comparison with other sales organizations leads you to believe that there are a number of areas in which improvements might be made. You decide to:

1. Enforce call-backs on old customers.
2. Require a minimum number of new customer calls, with the number depending on the salesperson.
3. Evaluate the success of the new customer calls.
4. Educate the sales force concerning the products that they sell.
5. Educate the sales force about successful sales techniques.
6. Build a sales force image and presence in the industry.

An evaluation of each salesperson is performed to establish a baseline for sales performance. A complete list of old customers is established for each salesperson, and the old customer lists are entered into the private information system. Each week, a schedule for visiting the old customers is produced for each salesperson. In addition, the private information system is used to notify each salesperson of the expected number of new customer calls to be performed during the week.

On a daily basis, each salesperson enters the sales information, the number of contacts with old and new clients (prospects), and the value of sales, into the private information system. On a weekly and on a monthly basis, the performance of the individual salespeople is monitored and the salespeople are ranked in the critical categories. The salespeople who are performing well are invited to make presentations at the weekly sales staff meetings to explain their successful techniques. Part of the weekly sales meetings are also devoted to education on both old and new products.

An examination of the successful sales factors is made, and individual salespeople are encouraged to try them. An industrywide examination of successful sales factors is performed, and the most promising are selected for trial in your group. After the testing period, the most successful factors are incorporated into your sales standards. Your choice of factors includes appearance, product knowledge, technical support, punctuality, and language expression. Having selected the characteristics that you consider critical for your salespeople to have, you modify your private information system to help you determine the effects of the new sales techniques. Discreet contacts are made to both new and old customers to determine the reasons for the successes and failures of your salespeople. The information that directly impacts your salespeople is used to fine tune both your managerial techniques and the techniques of your sales force. The critical success factors by which you are judged as a manager are carefully monitored by your private information system, and any trends that indicate anything other than steady progress are immediately investigated and corrective action is taken.

An evaluation of the reasons for successes and failures has led to specific product information, as well as to information about sales techniques. A simple statistical analysis yields information on the product features most liked and most disliked by old and potential customers. Specific information on reputation and the product features that led to success or failure of sales is passed on to your superiors. Modifications are made in production to enhance the good features and to remove or deemphasize the undesirable features of the products that you sell. As a result, sales figures go up again and you get the credit for it.

9.3 The Raw Materials Inventory Manager

You have just been assigned to head the raw materials inventory department. The economy is currently in decline, and high-level management has asked you to find some way to reduce the total investment in the inventory, but you must have enough materials on hand for production. The instructions from high-level management are rather vague, but it is clear that you must do something fast.

You use the organization's information system to determine seasonal trends in needs for raw materials. Historical information from the last economic decline is examined in an attempt to determine past patterns of needs for raw materials during a decline. In your department, you locate workers who have been in inventory for at least 10 years and get their predictions for the raw material needs for the next year. You then examine the current process for ordering and warehousing raw materials and discover that it is based on the "ideal quantity on hand" reordering system. An ideal quantity has been determined for each item. When the quantity on hand drops below the ideal quantity, an order is placed for the amount that will bring the amount on hand up to the ideal quantity.

Seasonal patterns in retail sales and the desire to keep inventory as low as possible, but still be able to support manufacturing in an appropriate manner, lead you to believe that significant reductions in inventory on hand can be achieved through a carefully planned ordering system. For some items you use seasonally adjusted, ideal quantities. Some items will be ordered only on a demand basis. Some items are marked for deletion from inventory. These items will be sold when an appropriate bid is obtained. Meanwhile, efforts are made to find purchasers for these items. Inventory will be examined on a periodic basis to verify that the reorder type and amount is appropriate for each item. The ability to make adjustments is built into the modifications to the information system that you request.

You decide to treat the inventory department as a system affected by its environment. Since the economy is in decline, housing starts have dropped off and the supply of copper is unusually high. As a result, the price for copper is unusually low. Your organization uses large amounts of copper on a regular basis, so you decide to stockpile copper, buying when it is cheap and using it as necessary. Over the period of a year, your innovative and flexible ordering techniques have saved the organization a substantial amount of money.

9.4 The Purchasing Department

You are the manager of purchasing. Even though you have received assurances from your subordinate managers that they are following company purchasing policies, you have the suspicion that materials cost the organization substantially more than they should. Reason tells you that the problems, if there really are any, would exist in either the bid process or in the awarding of purchase orders. There is a book from which names of vendors are drawn for the purpose of requesting bids, but it is not reasonable to try to trace every purchase order back to the bid process to determine if proper procedures were followed.

Your first step is to install an optical scanner for all bids. When a vendor enters a bid, the representative of the vendor enters it in person on a specially prepared form using an approved print font. The representative of the vendor verifies that the bid has been entered correctly immediately after the bid has been entered. Each bid is recorded by the computer that is connected to the scanner. Once a bid has been entered through the scanner and it has been approved by the representative of the vendor, it cannot be changed. The next step is to enforce bidding standards.

Names of vendors and their past performance ratings are entered into a computerized file. The selection of vendors for bids on specific items is done by the computer, following an algorithm designed by the purchasing department. The names of additional vendors can be added to the list produced by the computer, if the manager of bids so desires. Bids from vendors will be accepted only if their name appears on the list originally produced by the computer, as amended by the bid manager. The evaluation of the bids is performed by someone not under the bid manager. It is expected that this new separation of functions will help ensure that the award process is not biased.

The evaluation of the bids is performed by a combination of the computer and selected personnel. The computer ranks the bids according to an algorithm based upon the following criteria:

1. The closeness of the type and quality of the offered item to the desired item.
2. The closeness of the proposed delivery date or schedule to the desired delivery date or schedule.
3. The closeness of the quantity that can be delivered with the quantity desired.
4. The unit price for the item.

The bids are ranked by the computer in a number of ways. If the bid contains no deviation in type, quality, or delivery from the specifications in the request for bid, then the bids are ranked strictly by unit price. Each bid that contains a deviation of any kind is ranked against all other bids that contain a deviation of the same kind. Multiple deviations are noted on each ranking report. The personnel who make the final determination of the vendor may select the best bidder from the "no deviation" list without further justification. If any other vendor is selected, a justification of the selection must be made by the person making the selection, and this must be entered into the information system. A report of all selections is given to you or to your designee on an exception basis: if the best bidder on the "no deviation" list is not selected, then the selection, including the justification for the selection, is reported.

Even though each person involved in the bid and award process states that all of the departmental regulations had been followed in the past, the use of the information system to control these two processes leads to a substantial reduction in purchasing costs.

9.5 Property

You are the manager of a property company. You are using all of the accepted methods to sell houses, but you find that you have many more houses for sale than you do customers. A new approach is needed. You have been advertising in local newspapers in the standard, accepted manner, but sales are still too low. You decide to examine both the advertisements and the buyers on the chance that a certain type of advertisement leads to a higher percentage of sales.

The individual advertisements used by your company and by your most successful competitors are examined for their identifying characteristics. Comments and suggestions are solicited from sales and office personnel. A simple correlation of individual and groups of advertisement characteristics is performed. The computer is important here because it can perform the correlations quickly and easily, varying the number of characteristics examined each time.

Some obvious characteristics, such as the size, shape, and graphic layout of the advertisement, appear to be important in the success of sales. In addition, some unsuspected relationships arise. From your examination, you determine that certain wording of advertisements should be associated with certain neighborhoods and price ranges. You must make the advertisement match the characteristics of the potential buyers and not use one type of advertisement for all types of houses in all areas.

Now that you have identified a previously unknown characteristic of successful advertisements, you discuss with satisfied buyers what part of your advertisements attracted them. You start to build a store of phrases and information concerning distinct neighborhoods and price ranges. After trying a number of combinations, you fine tune your private information system to automatically produce descriptions to be applied to houses in specific neighborhoods and in specific price ranges. When you enter the basic, plain language description of the house, the price, and the neighborhood, your private information system prints a sample description for an advertisement incorporating the appropriate phraseology.

9.6 Receivables

Your organization manages a chain of large truck stops, and you have responsibility for the collection of receivables. There is a considerable amount of credit card usage by transport companies since they will not let their drivers carry large amounts of cash. Lorries from one company can charge tens of thousands of pounds in just one month. You have several concerns, including: (1) collection of past due receivables, (2) stopping charge activities by lines more than 60 days in arrears, and (3) stopping charge activities by lines that have filed for bankruptcy.

Your first thought is to have the technical personnel in your information systems department immediately write the programs that you need and to include an automatic charge rejection for the accounts that are overdue and for those that have filed for bankruptcy. When you contact the information systems department, you are told that personnel will be assigned to your problem just as soon as possible. In fact, you will be given the highest priority for the very next available person. Further investigation reveals that the expected availability of a programmer will be in about 30 days. You are already familiar with the organization's query system, so you decide to use it instead of waiting for a programmer. A delay of 30 days could cost your organization tens of thousands of pounds.

You use the query facility of your organization's information system to list the names, addresses, and dollar amounts owed for all accounts more than 30 days in arrears. The report also lists the amount due in each of the over-30-, over-60-, and over-90-day categories. All charge activity is immediately stopped for accounts 60 days overdue, and a concerted action is started to recover these receivables. If an account is 30 days overdue, the appropriate person is contacted for payment, and the organization is notified that further charges will not be accepted unless payments are made to reduce the over-30-day amount to zero. The query system is also used to notify individual truck stops of the names and accounts of shipping lines that are not allowed to make further charges.

Once the new plan has been implemented and fine tuned to your satisfaction, you request that your new operations be incorporated directly into the organization's information system.

The reasons for using the query system on the organization's computer are: (1) all of the necessary data is already in the organization's information system, (2) the query system allows you to do just what you need to accomplish, in a timely and efficient manner, and (3) you can fine tune your approach as needed.

9.7 Accounting

A number of your workers are responsible for updating computerized journals and ledgers. Some workers perform their tasks manually to verify the correctness of their entries, and then they enter the information into the organization's information system. Other workers enter their information directly into the journals and ledgers. An investigation reveals that many workers find the organization's computerized system too hard to use. If they make a mistake, the process of correction is just too cumbersome and time consuming. In addition, the computerized system has been slowed down by the frequency of error correction, i.e., the number of entries that must be corrected has grown so large that the entire system has been slowed down. When users hit the return or enter key of their terminal, a wait of 10 seconds is not unusual. Having to wait 10 seconds is very frustrating to the users of the system.

You recognize the problem as arising from the outdated design of the accounting system. High-level management is reluctant to have the entire accounting system rewritten, for if it were, it would take too much time and money to verify that the new system operates correctly, and current operating schedules would be disturbed. High-level management knows that the current system works correctly, and they consider a slow but correctly working system to be acceptable.

It is clear that the problem cannot be solved through authorized modifications to the organization's information system, so you purchase a number of microcomputers for your office, together with specialized software and communication equipment. Now your workers enter the journal and ledger information into the microcomputers and then verify the correctness of their entries right on this computer. Once the verification has been completed, the actual journals and ledgers within the organization's computerized system are updated by sending the information directly from the microcomputers to the organization's computer. The total amount of time required of each worker has been reduced since the data is entered only once (into the microcomputer), and the individual microcomputers are both more friendly and faster than the organization's computer. In addition, frustration derived from error correction has been reduced, reliability has been increased, and the capacity of the organization's computerized system has effectively been increased.

Due to your initiative, the small investment in the microcomputers and the communication equipment has led to a low-cost solution to a significant problem. You also solved the problem within the parameters established by high-level management since the current information system does not have to be rewritten. An additional bonus is that an unnecessary load has been removed from the current organizational information system, so the large, expensive, organizational computer is free to be used for other tasks.

9.8 Telephone Ordering

The telephone ordering portion of your sales has been steadily increasing over the last year. In the past, you have provided each of the people taking orders over the telephone with a listing of inventory that was accurate as of 5 P.M. the previous day. The previous day's listing is no longer reliable because the volume of orders in any one day may now completely exhaust your inventory, and some of your people may sell items over the telephone that your organization will not be able to deliver. Irate customers have let you know that your current methods are not adequate. At the current time your organization has no computer of its own.

Your first step is to contact the local university to buy time on their large time-sharing computer. You have determined that you cannot afford to purchase a large computer and write your own inventory control package, so you wish to reduce the cost through the use of a data management package on the university's computer. After you rent a small number of terminals and modems from the computer centre, everything is set up and ready to go. After using the university's computer for a month, you discover that you have two problems:

1. The computer becomes unavailable for extended periods of time. Sometimes this is due to hardware problems, sometimes the computer centre has a rush job to run at a higher priority than you have, and sometimes there are too many students using the system at any one time.

2. There are periods of time when the computer operates much too slowly for your needs. When a customer phones in, you cannot afford to wait five minutes for an update on the status of your inventory. Your customers expect fast service over the telephone.

You still desire to use the university's computer because of its expected cost savings, but you have to find some way to make your total system more reliable. Conversations with the director of the university's computer centre have proved fruitless. You might be able to live with a small number of computer hardware failures, if it doesn't take too long to fix the computer, but bad response time on a frequent basis cannot be tolerated.

You purchase a small number of microcomputers, a data management package, communication software, and modems. You have a choice of using the microcomputers in a number of different ways.

1. You can use the microcomputers to handle normal

business transactions and update the historical files at the university at night.

2. You can use the university's computer and data management system to handle the business transactions and use the microcomputers as an emergency backup. This will necessitate transfer of current inventory data from the university to the microcomputers on a regular basis.

3. You can terminate your agreement with the university, transfer all data to your microcomputers, and base your entire information system upon the microcomputers.

You realize that it will take time to implement your own information system (including the telephone ordering/inventory function), so you decide to continue using the university's computer and to have work started immediately on your own system. When your system becomes operational, you will test it out by running it in parallel with the system on the university's computer and in case the university's computer becomes too slow or unavailable. When you have confidence in your own system, you will switch the bulk of the operations to the microcomputers and will use the university's computer only for special research and for software that would be too expensive for you to buy or for software that is not available for your microcomputers.

Through the use of the microcomputers and the university's computer, you have increased both the speed and the reliability of the entire telephone ordering system. In addition, since the large historical files are kept on low-cost storage at the university, the cost of using the university computer is relatively small. You have plans to purchase your own (larger) computer later, if the volume of sales justifies this action. In the meantime you can use the university's facilities, including their data management package and their sophisticated statistics routines to analyze your sales figures and find creative approaches to increase sales.

9.9 Beef Herd Management

You manage a cattle ranch. In order to help you decide which cows to keep for breeding and which to sell, you currently use the services of a commercial beef herd management service. You record all of the calving information of interest and send it to the commercial service. Several months later you receive a series of reports that help you to determine which cows are good producers. The reports that you receive from the commercial service are almost what you want. For the most part they give you the information that you really need, but you would like some minor changes made in the reports. Unfortunately, the commercial service cannot make the changes that you requested since they have other customers that like the system just as it is. No problem. You can live with the reports the way they are.

There are two major problems with the service that you currently use: (1) You have no way to access certain kinds of historical information, so you cannot trace breeding lines through several generations. (2) You have to wait several months to receive the reports, and you need them considerably earlier than that.

You buy one microcomputer for your own use, hire a software technician, and have a close duplicate of the current beef herd improvement system created for your own use. The minor changes that you wanted are incorporated into your own system. The total cost of the system does not exceed $10,000, a sum that you expect to make up in a few years through improved herd management. You will now start to collect historical breeding information which you expect can be used to save you additional money.

You already have a suspicion that there are several other ranchers in the same position that you were in. After you test out your own beef herd management system, you contact several of the ranchers in your area and sell them a copy of your system. Within a year you find that you have completely paid for your entire system, both hardware and software.

9.10 The Fast-Food Restaurant

You are the owner of a fast-food restaurant. Even though you are part of a franchise operation, you are free to set whatever prices you need to for your food, except for nationally advertised sale items. Since the price of your food and paper items fluctuates and since your profit margin is quite small, you must keep a close watch on the prices that you charge. You notice that there are situations when you lose money during a month but don't know that there was a loss until two months later. If you could vary your prices to match actual food costs, then you feel that you would not lose money during any month.

Your first step is to design a system that will keep track of the average cost of every food item that you have. Each menu item is broken down into its separate components. For example, a hamburger consists of fixed-size portions of roll, meat, mustard, ketchup, pickles, and paper wrapping. The preparation cost, overhead, and profit are computed as a percentage of the food cost. Each time that you receive a shipment of food or paper items from your suppliers, you enter cost information into the system. On a regular basis you would like to print out a complete menu. The menu will contain a description of each item that you sell (like a hamburger or a cheeseburger) and the recommended selling price based upon average food and paper costs over the last three months. Since it is possible that there has been an unusual increase in the cost of the ingredients of a menu item, you would like the system to produce two prices: the price that represents the average cost of the ingredients over the last three months and the price that represents the ingredient costs from the last shipment.

You purchase a microcomputer and contract for the services of a software technician. The technician builds the system for you within a month. Your problem now is to determine when cost changes warrant price changes and how frequently to change your prices.

9.11 The Restaurant Menu Generator

You are the manager of a restaurant. You would like to spend more time directly supervising your employees, but you find that your office duties require more of your time than you would like. You spend so much time in the office that you do not have enough time to spend in the restaurant.

You examine how you spend your time and determine that there are several areas that take a considerable amount of your time: (1) ordering supplies, (2) verifying shipments of materials, and (3) planning the daily special. You already have a microcomputer in your office to help you with some of your work, like inventory control, so you decide how to expand the system that you have to give you more free time.

You plan a system to produce the purchase orders for you. The purchase orders are based upon the foods and other items that you want to have on hand and the suppliers of the items. The system will print out a suggested list of items to be ordered and will allow you to delete items from the list, add items to the list, or change the item counts. You may make whatever changes that you want to and then the system will print the completed purchase orders for you, one per supplier.

To reduce the amount of time that you spend verifying shipments from suppliers, you assign the task to the assistant manager, but you frequently visit with the assistant manager when a shipment is being verified in order to supervise this activity.

The daily special consists of two menu items: one for the noon meal and one for the evening meal. You now choose from a list of about 75 different specials, computing the cost of the special from the ingredients. You design a "specials menu" similar to the menu of 9.10 above, except that you use it to compute the price of the specials specifically chosen for the current day, and you want the system to print out a number of slips describing the specials of the day. The slips can then be clipped to the menus. You also decide to use this same system to help you determine the cost of banquets and other special meals.

You contact the software technician that built the inventory control system and contract for the two systems described above. Since you already have the microcomputer and the system development software, the cost of extending your current system is relatively small.

9.12 The Pharmacy System

You are a pharmacist. You find that you spend as much time typing labels and recording the sale of controlled substances as you do actually filling the prescription. You first write the specifications for an inventory system to keep track of all the items on your shelves, including the NDCC number, the item description, and the item cost. Then you write the specifications for a small system to enter the drug number (the NDCC number), the quantity, the number of refills, and the physician's name. The system will obtain the item description and any special instructions from your inventory files and present them on the screen. You want the opportunity to change or add to the special instructions. Once you have verified the contents of the label, the system will print the label, print the customer receipt, and update your inventory files. You would also like to have your new system automate your ordering procedures. You obtain the services of a good software technician to build the system for you on a contract basis.

When work is being done for you on a contract basis, you might agree to a fixed price for the entire application package or the software technician might work on an hourly basis. A fixed price for the package usually offers you greater protection than work done on an hourly basis. I also suspect that you will save money if you purchase your computer system and system development software from someone other than the software technician.

CHAPTER 10

A Case Study

10.1 Introduction

In this chapter, a single example is used to (partially) demonstrate the construction of a private information system. The example is given to illustrate some of the techniques presented in this book.

10.2 Background of the Loan Officer Case Study

A loan officer in a bank has the responsibility for all mortgage loans. In the past, this responsibility was entirely supported by the bank's information system. All mortgages were approved by the bank, and complete computerized records were kept concerning the mortgage. In particular, the bank's computer would produce a monthly list for all mortgages, showing the name, address, and payment status for all accounts not paid up to date. As payments were received, the amounts and dates of payment were entered into the system. The major inputs into the system were the original mortgage information and the monthly payments. The major output was the monthly list indicating accounts in arrears.

In recent years, the situation has changed. Individual mortgagees have, from time to time, found it necessary to make their own financial arrangements with buyers of their houses. After the mortgagee of record sells the property, the new buyer makes payments to the mortgagee, and the mortgagee makes payments to the bank. The bank considers the mortgagee of record to have total responsibility for all payments.

Since timely payments are of paramount importance to the bank, the bank has suggested to the mortgagees of record that the bank act as a collector of payments from the new buyers, and that the bank directly apply the payments received to the loans. When this was first proposed to the mortgagees, the number of accounts handled in this manner was quite small, approximately 25. Over the last few years, the number of accounts affected by this type of "creative" financing has grown to more than 500 and has become unmanageable.

10.3 The Current Processing

Upon examination of the current system (mode of operation), the loan officer determines each of the following:

1. For each buyer, a separate, noncomputerized loan record is established. This record contains the name and account number of the mortgagee, the name and account number of the buyer, and a payment schedule for the buyer.
2. When a payment is received by the bank from a buyer (not a mortgagee), John (a clerk) examines the buyer's loan schedule and enters the payment in the noncomputerized record.
3. The amount of the payment from the buyer is entered into a separate account for the mortgagee.
4. When, according to the payment schedule for the mortgagee, a payment by the mortgagee is due, Mary (another clerk) withdraws the required amount from the separate account and enters the amount as an ordinary payment.
5. If funds in the separate account are not sufficient

for the required payment, the mortgagee is sent an overdue notice.

The loan officer realizes each of the following:

1. The current system was set up in a hurry, so no consideration was given to finding a good solution to the original problem.
2. The current system is an "add on" system, i.e., the bank's computerized information system was not modified in any way to accommodate the collection service.
3. The collection service is entirely manual and has become too time consuming.

The loan officer feels that there should be some way to improve the situation in a cost effective manner.

10.4 Problems with the Bank's Information System

The loan officer contacts the Information Systems Department of the bank to start a preliminary dialogue about the problem. The loan officer soon understands that the Information Systems Department considers the problem to be small enough that a low priority would be assigned to the project (it would take at least a year before the Information Systems Department could start on the project); so, the loan officer decides to seek help elsewhere. The loan officer sees a good opportunity for visibility within the organization, writes down a number of ideas, and presents them to the vice president in charge of loans (the mentor). The vice president likes the idea of automating the system but cannot allocate the funds in advance, since it is contrary to bank policy to use non-bank resources. The vice president indicates that every effort will be made to reimburse the loan officer for costs incurred, if the project is successful. Encouraged by the vice president, the loan officer decides to use private funds to finance the project, if the total cost is under £5,000.

10.5   Obtaining the Services of a Software Technician

The loan officer advertises in a local newspaper for a software technician. The ad specifically states that the candidate must be able to perform all of the tasks associated with, and have experience in, the construction of an information system. The project is described as small and is to be performed on a microcomputer. The project is to be completed on a contract basis, i.e., the successful candidate will describe in writing how the project will be accomplished and will receive a fixed amount for the project.

Several candidates apply and are interviewed by the loan officer. The following criteria are used to screen the candidates:

1. At least a bachelor's degree in computer science or information systems.
2. A good knowledge of the modern techniques of analysis, design, and programming.
3. Training and experience in the construction of information systems.
4. Knowledge of both microcomputer hardware and software.
5. Knowledge of microcomputer to mainframe communications.

After each candidate is screened, the candidate is presented with a written description of the problem and is asked to present a proposal for a solution. The proposal is to contain an outline of the solution method and an approximate cost for the project.

The proposals are compared both with each other and with the loan officer's estimation of the situation, and one of the candidates is selected for the project. At this time, the software technician is asked for a fixed amount for the project, based upon the specifications (criteria) that were drawn up by the loan officer. The amount is to include the cost of the computer, a modem, a printer, the software, and the services of the software technician. The cost of the project is broken down as follows:

IBM XT SDD (Mono) with 640K memory and two disc drives	£1,865
Graphics printer	385
Printer cable	40
Services	1,000
System development software	900
Communications software	150
Total	£4,340

In addition, the final proposal contains a list of all of the functions that the private information system is to perform. Since the total cost of the project is under £5,000, the loan officer decides to go ahead with the project.

10.6   The Analysis

The software technician has a good idea concerning the nature of the problem to be solved but knows that the way John and Mary see their jobs may differ from the way in which the loan officer sees the same jobs. In fact, there is some slack in the £1,000 fee for services to take this into account. The software technician carefully interviews the loan officer to verify that the criteria for the private information system are well understood. The next step is to interview John and Mary. At this stage, all data concerning the bank's information system comes from the loan officer's department.

The software technician draws the diagram shown on the following page (Diagram 10.1) to describe the flow of data for the problem.

DIAGRAM 10.1

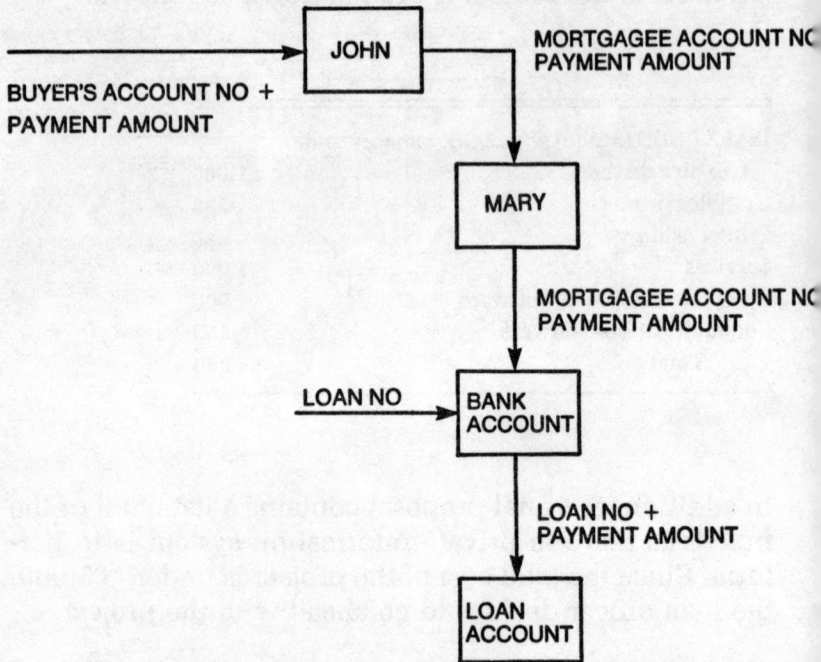

On the facing page is a refinement of Diagram 10.1, explicitly naming the functions. In Diagram 10.2, the data files are shown through the use of cylindrically shaped boxes.

The software technician then "fleshes out" the information derived from Diagram 10.2 and lists the following functions that the system must do: (1) enter payments from a buyer, (2) update the buyer account records, (3) transfer the payment to the mortgagee account, and (4) transfer the payment to the loan account.

Functions to be added to the system are: (1) back out a buyer payment, if the check used to make the payment does not clear, and (2) notify the mortgagee if the buyer is late with a payment or if a buyer's cheque does not clear.

DIAGRAM 10.2

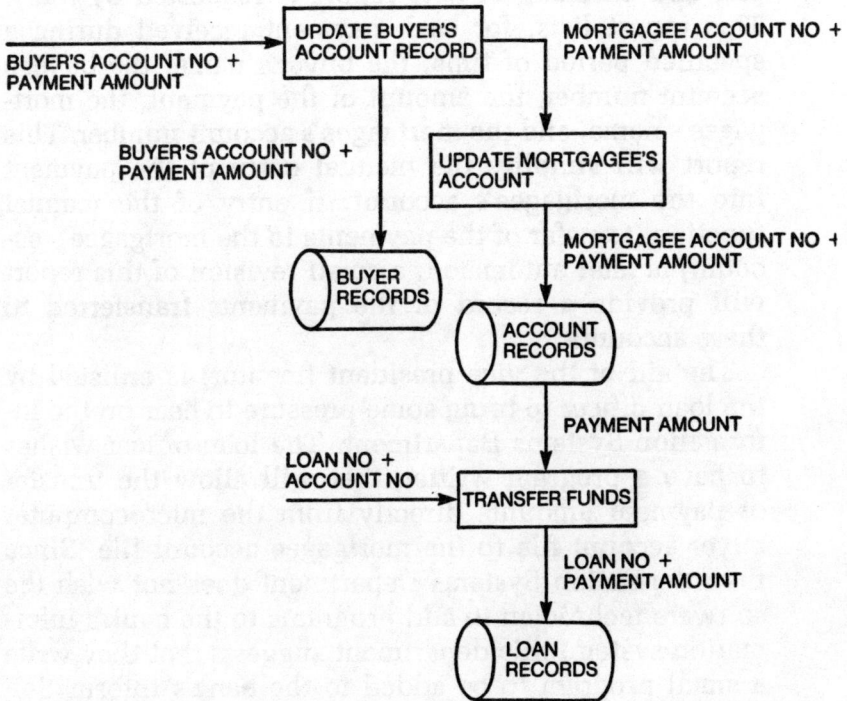

10.7 Design

The software technician identifies the major functions in conjunction with the loan officer, and the loan officer logically specifies how each of the functions is to operate. The software technician then designs the files and writes algorithms for each of the functions in the system.

10.8 Implementation

The original version of the system leaves updating of the mortgagee account and the loan records as manual processes since permission has not yet been obtained for direct access to these files. The system is tested and fine tuned so that the processing of the payments is easy, simple, and efficient. A new report is requested by Mary. This report lists, for each payment received during a specified period of time, the buyer's name, the buyer's account number, the amount of the payment, the mortgagee's name, and the mortgagee's account number. This report will simplify the manual entry of the payment into the mortgagee's account. If entry of the manual function (transfer of the payments to the mortgagee's account) is later automated, a small revision of this report will provide a record of the payments transferred to these accounts.

The aid of the vice president (mentor) is enlisted by the loan officer to bring some pressure to bear on the Information Systems Department. The loan officer wishes to have a program written that will allow the transfer of payment amounts directly from the microcomputer buyer account file to the mortgagee account file. Since the Information Systems Department does not wish the software technician to add programs to the bank's information system, this department suggests that they write a small program to be added to the bank's information system. The loan officer will send mortgagee account numbers and payment amounts to the bank's information system on a regular basis. The new program to be written by the Information Systems Department will take the account numbers and payment amounts and will update the mortgagee account records. The loan officer also suggests that a program be written by the Information Systems Department to transfer amounts from the mortgagee accounts to appropriate loan accounts. It is discovered that a minor modification of an existing funds transfer program already in the bank's information system will serve this purpose.

10.9 The Proposal

John and Mary now perform many of the tasks that they used to, but many of them are now automated by the new private information system. In addition, new reports produced by the system make some of the aspects of their jobs easier. Analysis of the new system reveals that John and Mary are much more satisfied with the type of work that they do and that they could easily handle 1,000 payments a month, if the number of buyer payments were to increase to that amount. The programs written for the loan officer by the Information Systems Department have also reduced the total load on the bank's computer since slow, interactive input of the payment data has been significantly reduced.

At this stage, the loan officer writes a proposal to the vice president in charge of loans. The proposal reviews the nature of the original problem, the steps taken to solve the problem, and the measurements that indicate that the implementation of the solution was a success. It is further proposed by the loan officer that the same type of system be installed in all of the branch offices of the bank. The proposal includes specific amounts for each system to be installed. Since the application software produced by the software technician is the property of the loan officer (this was stipulated in the agreement between the software technician and the loan officer), the total cost of each system to be installed will be approximately £3,200.

The vice president approves the proposal and passes the proposal up to the financial committee with an attachment recommending that the loan officer be commended for the work done, that the loan officer be in charge of the installation and training project, and that the loan officer be reimbursed for the original expenses of £4,340, with the bank becoming the owner of the hardware and associated software.

10.10 Discussion of the Case Study

The loan officer recognized the existence of a problem and realized that there was an opportunity for visibility. Groundwork was laid for the project in two ways: the loan officer performed a preliminary analysis of the problem before obtaining the services of a software technician, and the loan officer had already targeted a high-level manager both as a mentor/protector and as a recipient of a proposal.

The change in the bank's information system was necessitated by a change in the environment. The first approach by the bank's branch offices was to offer a new service to mortgagees, with all of the paperwork being performed manually. The loan officer recognized that the current procedures could be improved if they were automated and integrated with the bank's current information system. The private information system was the approach chosen by the loan officer to solve the problem.

A specific set of criteria was used to screen the candidates. The terms of the agreement between the chosen candidate and the loan officer were based upon the special circumstances of the project. For example, the services of the software technician were terminated when the private information system was accepted by the loan officer.

The loan officer, John, and Mary all participated in the analysis and the design of the system. In addition, the loan officer also wrote the specifications for each of the major functions in the system. The loan officer made the final decision as to which functions would be automated and which ones would be performed manually. The loan officer, John, and Mary all participated in testing and fine tuning the system.

John and Mary were retained to perform many of the same tasks that they had previously performed. They were not replaced by the partial automation of their tasks. The automation was instrumental in making their jobs easier and more productive.

The proposal was used to inform the vice president in charge of loans as to the degree of success of the new system. Armed with this information, the vice president was able to convince the financial committee of the bank not only that the new system was feasible, but also that providing each of the banks with a microcomputer might encourage managers at many of the branch offices to pursue the idea of a private information system. It was ex-

pected that the functions to be performed on the microcomputer would eventually be incorporated directly into
the bank's information system, freeing up the microcomputers and making them more widely available at each
branch.

CHAPTER 11

Packaging Proposals to Higher Management

11.1 Introduction

It is often the case that you will have to make your own successes visible. If this is the situation, be assertive but not offensive. You know your own successes better than anyone else, so you are in a good position to make them known. Your job is to make those successes visible so that you will be considered in a favourable light by high-level management. Just because you are successful does not guarantee that others will notice you. Higher-level management may be tied up in their own concerns, leaving you to float for yourself. It is also possible that you have worked as part of a group. In this situation, it will be necessary to clarify your participation in and your contributions to the group.

> You may need to make your own successes visible.

I once worked for an organization where small working groups were often formed to handle specific problems. No one was ever designated to head this type of working group. It was felt that leadership qualities would surface in a natural manner in such an arrangement. The advantage of working in such a group was that every member had an equal opportunity to display leadership and problem-solving abilities. No one, by virtue of appointment, could control the entire group. The disadvantages were that different personalities, different leadership techniques, and different problem-solving abilities would inevitably clash and that it was difficult for any single individual to achieve visibility. Either the entire group would succeed or the entire group would fail. The opportunities for individual visibility were therefore limited.

You might find yourself in a similar situation or in some other situation that makes you feel that you do not have the opportunities for visibility. You may feel that you do not have the opportunities to demonstrate your abilities or you may feel that you have demonstrated your abilities but no one has noticed. If this is the case, your plan for success must include not only the achievements themselves but also the selling of the achievements. You understand the environment in which you work. If it is common for achievements to go unnoticed in your organization, you must not only set recognition as one of your goals, but you must specifically plan how to obtain this recognition. Thus, when you plan your strategy, you must determine the specific problems to be solved, how you will solve the problem, and how you will make sure that you will be recognized for your achievements.

Include the selling of your achievements in your plan for success.

11.2 Target an Executive

Start by identifying a high-level manager. This individual may or may not be one of your direct superiors. Your task is favourably to impress this individual with your abilities to become a high-level manager yourself. If you can establish a good working relationship with such an individual, you will have both a protector and a mentor. A protector is someone who will look out for you and protect you when the going gets rough. More than one person has had his or her progress to a high-level management position stopped by someone already in high-level management merely because the high-level manager did not think that the individual was appropriate for the job or because the high-level manager was someone else's protector. A protector will fight for you, explain your talents and abilities to other high-level managers at appropriate times, and, if necessary, protect your special interests. A mentor is someone you can learn from. Although you may have the characteristics necessary for a high-level management position, you will probably still need some training to develop the requisite skills. When openings arise within high-level management, either within your organization or within some other organization, the recommendation of this individual may open the door for your advancement. The major problem here is that you must not put yourself in a position where you are just being used. Attempt to identify an individual with a reputation for total honesty and for loyalty to subordinates.

Select a high-level manager as a protector and mentor.

Remember that you are not trying to do favours for such a person and thereby earn return favours. You are seeking opportunities to learn new skills and to demonstrate your abilities. You may be in competition with other middle managers for the attention of this individual. Again, your task is to look as good as you can, not try to make others look bad. If you have properly prepared yourself, your abilities will be favourably compared with your competition, but even in competition you should help others to get ahead. For example, in sports such as hockey and basketball, assists for goals are considered to be almost as important as making the goals themselves.

In these same sports, the player who seeks only personal glory does not last long on the team.

One of the best ways to get the attention of a potential protector and mentor is to truly be useful to such an individual. Making this individual's job easier or making this individual look good as a result of your accomplishments will certainly help. When you plan your strategy, you might want to consider not only how to make yourself look good, but how you can contribute to making your immediate superior and your protector/mentor (if they are different individuals) look good. In most cases, making your superiors look good is much better than trying to look better than your superiors.

Put the needs of the organization first. Help others to get ahead, both your workers and your superiors.

11.3 Define the Problem that You Solved

Each of your successes must be carefully documented. The first step in the documentation is to define the problem that you have worked on and solved. This means that you must explain, in the most understandable terms, both the symptoms and the real nature of the problem. You are not just writing to impress others; you are writing to help others understand just what you have accomplished. Making your contributions understandable is one of the keys to success. Your writing style should always be simple and factual. At this stage it is important for you to understand the difference between the symptoms of a problem and the real nature of the problem.

Learn to distinguish between the symptoms and the nature of a problem.

The symptoms of a problem are the indicators that a problem exists. The nature of the problem is a description of its cause. For example, a man goes to the doctor with a high fever. The fever is a symptom of the problem, not the problem itself. The reason that the fever is only a symptom is that knowledge of the existence of a fever does not tell the physician how to treat the man. The reason for the existence of the fever, i.e., the underlying illness, is often the problem. Sometimes it is necessary to trace symptoms back to the underlying problem. For example, a woman goes to a doctor complaining of dizziness. The doctor determines that the woman is not receiving the proper nutrition. The lack of proper nutrition may itself be just a symptom of a problem. If the woman is overly concerned about her weight and is not eating a reasonably balanced diet, it is possible that no amount of instruction concerning proper eating habits will solve the problem. The woman may follow the doctor's instructions for a while and then go back on the undernourishing diet again. The real problem might be the desire to diet. If the problem is severe enough, as with anorexia nervosa, the real problem may be psychological in nature. Understanding the nature of the problem usually helps you to determine one or more reasonable solutions. In the case of a fever, a specific antibiotic may be prescribed. In the case of anorexia nervosa, specific psychiatric help may be needed.

One reason that identifying the real nature of the problem is so important is you must make sure that you have solved the actual problem, not just treated some of the symptoms. If you have actually solved the problem, it is highly unlikely that it will occur again. If you have only treated the symptoms, and have done so in such a way that the underlying problem has not been solved, then the problem will undoubtedly occur again. As an example, consider shortages in cash received. The shortage itself is just a symptom of the problem. One way of treating the symptom is to adjust the amount of cash received each time there is a shortage. This makes the books balance, giving the appearance of solving the problem, but the problem will probably occur again. If the problem is carelessness on the part of the cashier, action must be taken to make the cashier more careful. One possible technique is to make the cashier spend extra hours at work tracking down the error and correcting it. If the problem is that someone is taking money from the register, then another approach is needed. The approach used to solve the problem is often directly dependent upon the real nature of the problem. If you only treat symptoms, you can never be sure that you have really solved the problem. If you claim to have solved a problem and the same problem subsequently reappears, your integrity, judgment, and abilities will be in question.

> You must understand the real nature of a problem in order to solve it properly. You must be able to explain both the problem and your solution so that others can understand it.

As you move up through the ranks of middle management, the examination of your personal judgment will become more minute. Your understanding of the true nature of problems will have a considerable impact on your personal judgment for, the better you understand a problem, the better your judgments concerning the problem will be. Personal judgments enter into practically every phase of problem solving, from recognizing the existence of a problem to deciding how to present your solution to your superiors.

> As you progress through the ranks of middle management, your judgments will come under close scrutiny.

> The validity of your judgments is often based upon your understanding the nature of the problems that you face.

11.4 Detail the Background of the Problem

The evaluation of your work by high-level management is easier if you describe the environment or context of your work. You must not assume that high-level management will understand your work as well as you do. You have done the pioneering work. You invested a considerable amount of time and energy on the problem, so you understand it well now, but your understanding of the problem has evolved over a period of time. Others must now try to understand the problem. They will start where you did, trying to follow the paths of understanding that you followed. Now you must help others to understand the problem. Make the task of understanding the problem and its solution as simple as possible. If you can develop the ability to make difficult topics easy to understand, you will increase the probability of recognition.

Do not assume that high-level management understands the problems as well as you do.

Develop the ability to make difficult topics easy to understand.

Do not be too concerned with trying to look impressive. Some managers try too hard to make their achievements look impressive, and such an attempt can be self-defeating. Looking impressive is fine, as long as you do not make it difficult for others to either understand or appreciate your achievements. If others cannot understand what you have accomplished or if you offend them in your efforts to achieve recognition, then you will diminish your chances of reward. If you are faced with the decision of trying to look impressive or making your work understandable, strive first for clarity and understanding.

> Clarity and understanding are more important than looking impressive.

Clarity is often a matter of organization and writing style. Understanding usually follows from providing the background of the problem, a description of the nature of the problem, a description of the solution, and a description of why your choice of a solution really solves the problem. If you provide sufficient information for high-level management to evaluate your work, then you will have to spend less time justifying it. Work toward a strong presentation. Do not leave gaps in the development of the problem and its solution. Strive for a cohesive presentation in which each step logically follows the previous ones, and in which all of the parts fit together. Start with a proper foundation, the background of the problem, then develop the presentation, and end with the measurements of your successes.

> A clear presentation requires fewer justifications.

11.5 Describe Your Approach

It is important for high-level management to understand how you achieved your successes. They want to verify that your solution really works. In order to do this, they need to understand both the nature of the problem and the nature of the solution. If they can understand how you developed your solution, they can probably understand why your choice of a solution really works. This means that you must not be too technical in your presentation. Most of the high-level managers in your organization will not have the background to understand the details of the solution of a complex problem. An accountant will not understand the details of a solution to a manufacturing problem, and an engineer will not understand the solution to an accounting problem. You must present the material on both a technical and a conceptual level. Then a high-level manager with a background in your field can use the technical part of your presentation to aid in understanding, and the others can use the conceptual part of your presentation. Again, you must strive for clarity and understanding.

Help high-level management understand why your solution works.

Most of the time, if you attempt to detail each part of your approach, you will either bore your audience or lose them in the mass of detail, so you must come to grips with this problem. You should strive to hit the truly meaningful highlights. In the main part of your presentation, cover just enough material so that understanding is achieved, i.e., so that your audience can understand what you did and why you did it. Go into detail only when you are asked to do so. It will be difficult to find a level of detail appropriate for each member of your audience since the background of each individual will vary. Strive to have a reasonable balance between brevity and clarity, providing specific details upon request to the interested parties.

Strive for a balance between brevity and clarity in your presentation. Include enough detail so that the reader or listener can grasp the essentials, but not so much detail that the presentation will be boring.

11.6 Detail Your Successes

While you must be brief in the presentation of your problem-solving approach, you must be detailed in describing your actual successes. You must have a basis for measuring the performance of both the new and the old methods, i.e., the performance before and after you have made modifications. The particular measuring technique that you use must be the same for both the current performance and the previous performance. The ability to clearly demonstrate the superiority of the new methods over the old ones is absolutely critical. There are several problems associated with this part of your presentation: (1) the audience must understand the measurement techniques that you have employed, (2) they must feel that the measurement techniques are reasonable, (3) they must understand what your figures (measurements) mean, (4) they must understand the consequences of the figures, and (5) they must trust your integrity.

Items 1 and 2 will depend, to some degree, upon the background of the audience. Items 3 and 4 will depend upon how well you present the major concepts and upon how well you detail the consequences of your successes. You must be particularly definitive when discussing item 4. Item 5 is important because, if they do not trust your integrity, they may have a suspicion that you are trying to fool them. If they do not have complete confidence in you, they may require that a certain amount of time be allowed to elapse in order to verify that your conclusions are correct. Even worse, if they do not trust you, they may require that you go back to the old way of doing things. Since the evaluation of your work will depend to a great degree upon your reputation for honesty and integrity, you should set the achievement of this reputation as one of your major goals, and you should start working toward this goal immediately.

Use understandable techniques to measure your successes. Never be vague in your measurements or in your expectations.

If you develop a reputation for absolute honesty and integrity, others are more likely to believe your claims of success.

11.7 Propose a New Plan

Not only must you verify that your ideas will benefit the organization, but you must also present your ideas in a manner that will convince high-level management that it would be beneficial to implement these ideas. One technique that you might use is to present high-level management both with a record of the achievement in a limited area and with a plan for the actual implementation on a widespread basis. If you choose this approach, your plan should be clear and concise. You should have an implementation timetable, and you should be able to detail both the costs and the expected benefits associated with the implementation. Another reason for you to think about an implementation of your ideas is that, if your ideas are considered favourably by higher-level management, you are the logical choice to implement them. Another reason for your thinking about the implementation considerations is that higher-level management will always want to know each of the following: (1) What will be the immediate (up front) cost of implementing your ideas? (2) What additional resources will be necessary? (3) How much time will the project take? and (4) What will be the expected return on the investment? You will be able to answer questions 1 through 3 if you have carefully considered the implementation of your ideas.

> Be prepared to present a detailed plan for the implementation of your ideas.

There is one significant danger associated with the proposal of a plan for the implementation of your ideas. Even though you may have identified the real nature of the problem and have detailed a good solution to the problem, it is still possible to plan a poor implementation. Problem solving often occurs in four steps: (1) recognition of the existence of a problem, (2) understanding the real nature of the problem, (3) deriving a good solution to the problem, and (4) deriving an implementation of the solution. Each of these steps is independent of the others, in the sense that you may be good at doing some of them and still be poor at doing the others. The implementation of a good idea (solution) may be much more difficult than you might expect it to be.

> You might have solved a problem correctly and still have difficulty implementing it.

There may be a number of reasons that would cause you to have some difficulties implementing your ideas, including:

1. **A lack of technology.**

   The first attempts at the creation of the modern computer were hampered by the technology. The first computers of this century used electromagnetic relays. This technology was then followed by the vacuum tube and finally by the transistor. The use of the transistor in the modern computer made the computer both fast and reliable. The idea for the computer was there long before the technology was available to make it feasible.

2. **A lack of resources.**

   If the implementation of your ideas requires a considerable investment, it may take time to obtain the necessary people, equipment, and funds. In addition, the larger the amount of resources required, the greater the scrutiny on the part of high-level management to verify that your implementation should actually work. If the initial investment is too large, even if the expected returns are also large, the project may be tabled as impractical.

3. **A lack of proper planning.**

   It is easy to overlook the importance of the careful planning of the implementation. If you rush into the implementation without careful prior planning, you may find that the total amount of time and money required for the implementation is much greater than you had originally expected. It is also possible to choose a course for implementation that will guarantee that the project will fail. If schedules are too tight, you might drive critical people away. If you attempt to add too many people to the project, you might extend rather than shorten the time required for the completion of the project.

4. **Difficulty in dealing with some individuals.**

Every time that you attempt to do something new, you will find individuals who will oppose you. There is a certain inertia that must be overcome before new ideas are accepted. You may also find that powerful people in your organization oppose you. Their reasons may have either a political or an emotional basis. Some people just don't like to see others get ahead unless they can obtain some advantage from it. It is also possible that you have made some enemies you were not aware of. The fact that you have a protector can be very helpful in this kind of situation.

You must also take into consideration the feelings of those affected by the changes. Whenever new ideas are implemented, some people will wonder if the changes will force them out of work. Anyone with these feelings will be reluctant to participate in bringing about the changes. Thus, as part of the implementation plan, you must communicate with these individuals. If jobs are to be eliminated, you should have a plan for the affected people. It is usually better to use the affected people in other capacities in the organization, rather than to fire them or to lay them off. If it is not reasonable to expect that a new position can be found in the organization for each person affected, then your implementation plan should include specific help for these individuals, and the cost of this help should be included in your budget.

11.8 A Final Word on Proposals

Your proposal should be able to stand on its own merits and should be complete enough so that the average reader will be able to understand your ideas. Ordinarily, there should not be a need for high-level management to ask you for anything other than a small number of minor clarifications, although some high-level managers may occasionally ask for more details. You are now faced with a problem: How do you present your ideas so that you can keep the attention of your readers and still provide sufficient depth?

To solve this problem, I recommend that you write your proposal in more than one part, presenting your ideas in a top–down fashion. The first part of your proposal, in which you briefly describe all of the salient information, should be very short (just one page, if possible). The purpose of the first part of the proposal is to quickly catch the attention and the interest of the reader. The second part of the proposal should contain enough information to explain and justify the major ideas presented in the first part. The level of detail of the second part should be just barely sufficient to achieve this purpose. The third part should contain the remainder of the details, particularly those details that would be of interest only to a small percentage of your readers, but whose inclusion are necessary for completeness.

Your proposal should not only sell your ideas but should also sell your abilities. Put as much creative thought into your proposals as you do into the problems that you solve. Always dress up your presentations and proposals so that they appear to be professional in nature. A presentation or proposal represents a problem to be solved. Determine the goals to be achieved by the presentation or proposal, determine the kinds of problems that you might have in achieving these goals, derive reasonable solutions to these problems, and implement your solutions. Further visibility is often the reward for a well-constructed, attractive proposal.

CHAPTER 12

Putting It All Together

This chapter is an integrated summary of many of the major topics previously presented in this book.

12.1 The Strategy

To make it to a high-level management position, you must have a strategy. One way to create your strategy is to treat advancement to a high-level management position as an ordinary problem to be solved. Examine the problem to discover its real nature and determine, in a general sense, the objectives that must be accomplished in order to reach your end goal of a high-level management position. Build a unified plan to achieve these objectives, but make sure that achieving your objectives will either gain the end goal or will allow significant progress toward it.

Survey of Desired Characteristics

Examine the entire problem before you take any specific action, determining not only the problem itself but also the environment of the problem. Since each organization will present its own unique environment for the problem of advancement to a high-level management position, you will need to examine the problem within the context of its environment, the organization itself. Examine the successes of others who have made it to a high-level management position, both inside and outside your organization. Analyze the reasons for their successes and determine their specific achievements, their personal characteristics, and their abilities. Make a list of the common characteristics and abilities, and categorize the achievements. Once you have determined the kinds of achievements that lead to high-level management positions, see if you can correlate the characteristics and abilities with the achievements. Finally, determine the personal characteristics and abilities that you feel you will need to have and to display. Examine your list of characteristics and abilities. If honesty, integrity, and loyalty to superiors and subordinates are not on your list, add them. Delete any characteristics that would conflict with honesty, integrity, or loyalty.

Assessment of Current Characteristics

Make a list of your own characteristics and abilities. Be honest with yourself, but be fair. You may have the tendency to credit yourself both with some characteristics and abilities that you don't have and to feel that you don't have some that you really do. We all have difficulty seeing ourselves clearly. Seek the advice of those you trust to help you see yourself more clearly. Your spouse and co-workers may be helpful in this endeavour. Another approach is to examine the evaluations of your work by your superiors since their comments on your abilities will be most helpful to you. If you feel that your superiors have misevaluated or misjudged your personal characteristics and abilities, then either they or you are correct. If they are correct, you will need to add more items to your list. If you are correct, you must find some way to bring them to the attention of your superiors. In either event, you will need to treat them as characteristics or abilities to be gained and properly displayed.

Identification of Characteristics to Be Obtained

Once you have completed your examination of the kinds of characteristics and abilities that successful high-level managers have displayed and you have determined your own characteristics and abilities, make a list of those that you want to expand or obtain. Since you are a middle manager, you must already have most of what you will need. It is usually a matter of degree, rather than having or not having a characteristic or ability. For example, you may have a great deal of difficulty making clear and coherent presentations to your superiors because you are nervous in their presence. But you do not have this trouble when you are dealing with your subordinates, so you do have the basic ability to make clear and coherent presentations. You merely have to extend your abilities.

Some characteristics and abilities will be very easy for you to obtain or develop, and others will require both careful planning and considerable effort on your part. For example, in your organization, a particular degree or a degree from a particular school may be required. If this is the case, then careful, long-term planning will be required. Do not become discouraged either by the number or by the degree of difficulty of obtaining the characteristics and abilities that you feel you must acquire. Many of them are interrelated, so if you obtain a number of them, you will automatically obtain the remainder of them. A task always looks hardest just before you start it. Once you get into it and have some successes, achieving the final goal will seem much more reasonable.

Identification of Personal Goals

Before you can devise a plan, you must determine a specific set of goals to be accomplished. Include in this set of goals the characteristics and abilities that you wish to obtain and their display to high-level management. In some cases, a major goal is too hard to achieve in one step, so it is profitable to break up each of these major goals into a collection of subgoals. These goals should have the property that attaining them will lead directly to attaining the major goals. Continue to break up each difficult goal into a collection of simpler goals, until you feel that each of the goals at the lowest level is attainable. The process of breaking up a complex goal into a collection of simpler goals not only makes the overall task easier, but it also helps you to better understand what you have to do to advance to a high-level management position.

As you advance along the path to a high-level management position, you may need to make some modifications to your set of goals. Like any problem that you attempt to solve, your understanding of the problem will evolve over a period of time. Don't be too rigid either in the goals that you set for yourself or in your plans. Look for opportunities to bypass several steps that you have set for yourself to achieve a major goal. You may also find that some major goals do not have to be achieved or that you may have to add new ones.

Selection of a Protector/Mentor

Look around your organization for someone who can help you achieve your goals. This individual must have more power in the organization than you do and must be willing to help you. This person can provide two invaluable services for you: the first is to teach you much of what you need to know, especially concerning the unique environmental aspects of your organization, and the second is to look out for your interests.

You must earn the respect of this individual through solid achievement. Do not attempt to earn favours in return for favours that you do. The return of favours does not foster a relationship based upon mutual respect but tends to strengthen your role as a subordinate rather than as a potential equal. Identify and target a person who has a reputation for loyalty and helpfulness to subordinates. It is not necessary that this individual be a direct superior of yours, but the choice of a direct superior might be managers for the help of such an individual, but you must not try to make others look bad. If you help others to achieve, even those middle managers with whom you are in competition, you will increase your chances of receiving help yourself from a protector and mentor.

The role of a protector is to represent your interests at a level beyond your direct influence. There will be times when this representation will take the form of mentioning your name and accomplishments. In other cases, it may be to explain your actions or even to defend you. This is where the personal loyalty of your protector and mentor is important. When the going gets tough, your protector and mentor will need to have faith in you and your abilities.

You will not know the individual personalities of most of the high-level managers who will influence your progress within the organization. This is one kind of information that your mentor can provide to you. In addition, a good mentor can evaluate your potential for a high-level management position and make realistic suggestions for improvement. Each of us has several areas that need improvement. Since we cannot always see ourselves clearly, an evaluation by a mentor can be most helpful. A mentor can also steer a course for us so that we gain the right experiences and achieve appropriate visibility within the organization.

Targeting a High-Level Manager

There are actually two managers you will need to target: the protector/mentor and a direct superior. In some cases, these two individuals are the same person; in other cases, they are not. The direct superior will have the greatest influence as to your promotions. This individual must be convinced that you: (1) perform your current job in a good, if not outstanding, manner, (2) display more ability than other middle managers of the same rank, and (3) have the characteristics and abilities for a high-level management position.

This person must be in a position to either directly or indirectly recommend promotions for you. As you move closer to the top of your organization, the number of people from whom you can choose a direct superior will decrease. When there is only one direct superior above you, you cannot reasonably expect that this individual will recommend you for promotion, unless this individual will soon leave the organization either to retire or to join another organization. If your progress is stopped because there is not a place for you to go in your organization, it might be time for a move to another organization.

Survey of Organizational Goals and Methods

A basic part of the strategy is to learn as much about the organization as you can. Treat it as a system, and determine the role of your department within the system. Also study the historical development of your organization for goals and trends. Determine all of the current major goals of the organization, not just those that apply to your own department. Find out how each department within the organization contributes to the accomplishment of these goals. You wish to learn as much about the organization as you can so that you can determine the political realities of your environment and look for areas in which you might be able to achieve notable successes.

Survey of Departmental Goals and Methods

After you have completed your survey of organizational goals and methods, you should do the same for your own department. The first objective of this survey is to understand the role of your department within the organization (the systems approach). Determine the goals of your department and how these goals fit into the organizational goals. Examine the master plan for your department, examining it for strengths and weaknesses. Work your way down from the departmental goals and master plan, treating your own department as a subsystem within the organization. Determine the goals and master plan for each subdepartment, and establish how each subdepartment contributes to the goals of the department or subdepartment above it. The information that you gather from this survey will help keep you on track when you make changes within your department. You will, in general, not wish to make changes to the goals of your department. You will want to accomplish the existing goals more efficiently and will probably want to add new goals.

12.2 The Plan

Increase Your Personal Free Time

Make a list of all the things that you do. Note the times of the week, month, and year that they are done, the frequency with which each task is performed, and the amount of time it takes you to perform each task. Even if you have previously performed this survey, you might wish to do it again since work patterns often change over a period of time. Examine each of the tasks for their total demands on your time. You wish to determine which of your tasks require significant percentages of your time. The tasks that require much of your time are good candidates for delegation or for automation. *Your first concrete task under this plan is to significantly reduce the total demands on your time.* If you cannot reduce the demands that your job has on your time, then you will not be able to accomplish anything else. You must have new free time.

When you have increased your free time, you must make sure that you do not fill it with tasks directly associated with your current job. The total amount of work that you could conceivably do is always more than you can realistically do. You cannot reduce the total workload by working harder and longer because, if you do get caught up, you will simply be given more work to do. You must control your free time so that it can be devoted directly to accomplishing your personal objectives. Once you have some free time, you can: (1) take classes at a local university, (2) formulate detailed plans, (3) build a private information system, and (4) put specific efforts into the implementation of your plans. Without additional free time, you will have neither the time nor the energy for significant achievements.

The rules for obtaining free time are:

1. If a task can be done by someone else (a subordinate), then it should be.

2. If you delegate a task, make sure that the individual assigned to perform the task knows exactly how it is to be done. Allocate some of your time to instruct, supervise, and evaluate the work.

3. If you delegate a task that directly affects one of your critical success factors, i.e., one of the factors used by your superiors to evaluate your job performance, then you must monitor the performance of the task carefully. If the performance of a critical task falls below the desired level, then you must take immediate, personal action to raise the performance to an acceptable level. It might be appropriate to use your personal information system to help you monitor the performance of these critical tasks.

4. Search for tasks of a repetitive nature. If you can determine an algorithm for such a task, then it can be automated. The advantage of automating a task is that it will not place a significant burden on existing personnel. If an attempt to automate a task increases an individual's workload, then you must either reduce that person's current workload, hire another individual to perform the task, or not attempt to automate the task. It is almost always the case that the initial automation of a task will require extra effort on the part of an individual. For the same reason that you need to increase your free time, your subordinates will also need to increase their free time. You cannot expect them to continue to do their current jobs and find extra time to participate in the automation of a task unless you specifically help them. You may need to reallocate their workloads, provide additional (temporary) workers, or find some other means to help them.

Obtain the Services of a Software Technician

After you have a good idea of the kinds of things that you would like to do, you will need to obtain the services of a good software technician. This individual will need to have training and experience in the areas of analysis, design, and programming of information systems. Depending upon your circumstances, you might wish to hire such an individual directly or to obtain the loan of such an individual from another department within the organization. In most cases, you will need to hire such an individual yourself.

Look for someone with actual experience in all phases of the construction of information systems because this individual will need to work independently, but under your direction. You will need to rely on such an individual for advice and suggestions, and your skills and the skills of this individual must complement each other. The term *software technician* is not a standard one, but it is used in this book to describe an individual skilled in the three areas of analysis, design, and programming.

You are responsible for the overall design of the private information system since you understand the organization, the department, and your personal goals. The software technician is responsible for transforming your overall design into a specific, computerized, private information system. You must retain control of the total project in order to ensure that your goals will be achieved.

Do not attempt to obtain the services of a mediocre software technician, but look for someone with real skills. The worst thing that you can do is try to save money by seeking an individual who will accept the assignment for a low wage. Your entire future may rest on the quality of the private information system, so you want it to be as good as you can possibly make it. Also look for a software technician with social skills. The technician must be technically competent and also socially competent. This individual will have considerable contact with your subordinates, and it is most important that they respect this individual and feel comfortable. They must also know that they will not lose their jobs as a result of the efforts of the software technician.

Obtain Data Entry Services

You will probably need to enter data into your private information system on a regular basis. It is not reasonable to expect that someone who already has a full-time job will be able to make the time to enter the data. In addition, normal secretarial skills are not sufficient for data entry. Typing is not the same as data entry, and typing skills may actually make it difficult for someone to enter data. You must therefore assume that you will not be able to have a secretary enter the data for you.

Obtain the services of a skilled data entry person. If you have bad data entered into your private information system, it will have a detrimental effect upon the system. The typical error rate for a skilled data entry person is about 3 percent. Thus, for every 100 keystrokes (about the same as 100 characters of data), about 3 of them will be in error. A very good data entry person have an error rate of approximately 1 percent. You will find that most secretaries, because of their unfamiliarity with computers, constant interruptions, and typical typing techniques, will have an error rate in excess of 25 percent. You simply cannot afford a 25 percent error rate.

Pay as much attention to the selection of a data entry person as you do to the selection of a software technician. You will need professionals for both positions. Choose someone with training as a data entry specialist, preferably someone with some experience, although experience for a data entry person is not as critical as it is for a software technician. Before you have the data entry person actually enter the data, this individual should become thoroughly familiar with the operations of your department and the workings of your private information system. A number of problems can be eliminated if this individual knows what the data means and how it is to be used.

Obtain Permission to Access the Organizational IS

Part of constructing the private information system involves using the organization's information system to your advantage. Most of the time, official access to the information stored in the organization's information system is through formatted reports. You will need to gain direct access to the raw data itself so that you can use it to do your job the way that you want to. In order to gain direct access to the data, you will need specific permission of the owners of the data. If the data is treated as an organizational resource, you will need the permission of the database administrator. If the data is owned by individual departments, you will need permission of the departments concerned. In the second case, access may be considerably harder to obtain.

To access the data physically, you will either need a query system or your software technician will have to write programs for you. Since it may be difficult for you to gain permission to run your own programs on the organization's computer, you may be specifically limited to the use of the query system associated with the organization's information system.

Obtain a Microcomputer-Based Computing System

As the foundation of your private information system, you will need a microcomputer-based computing system. The system will consist of: (1) a microcomputer with one hard disk and one floppy disk drive, (2) a printer, (3) a modem, (4) communications software, and (5) a software development system.

I strongly recommend an IBM XT or compatible computer, with at least 320K main memory (640K is recommended), in order to guarantee availability of new software and the basic hardware features that you will need. Select a fast dot matrix printer (about 200 characters per second) that will accommodate wide paper and that will print at least 132 columns of output. The purpose of the modem and the communications software is to allow you access to the organizational information system. If your organization's information system will allow you access over a telephone line (and many of them do), you will be able to transfer data from the organization's computer to your own microcomputer as needed. The modem and communications software are necessary only if they can be used in this manner and if you have permission to access the data. The software development system will allow your software technician to build the specialized application system that you will need for your microcomputer-based private information system.

The specific software used for communications and for software development should be left to the software technician but should also be selected because it is best for your needs, rather than because of any previous usage of the software by the technician. A good software technician will be familiar with at least one kind of software, and that software is often suitable for your specific needs. The problem of which software to select arises when you have a software technician who does not have quite enough experience.

Perform a Survey of the Departmental Information Flow

Once you have reduced the demands upon your own time, you can reinvest it in other endeavours. If you wish to improve the performance and efficiency of your department, you will need to understand it first. Do not assume that you know everything there is to know about your own department. The department, like any living organism, changes over a period of time.

Use the skills of your software technician to perform a survey and an evaluation of the flow of information within your department. List all of the information that flows into your department, all of the information that is generated by your department, how the information is used within your department, and the recipients of information that your department passes on to others. Try to understand your department as an information consumer, generator, and processor.

Perform a Survey of the Departmental Work Procedures

As part of the evaluation of your department, examine the tasks of each of the workers in your department. Again, the skills of your software technician will be helpful here. Once you understand the nature of each task and how the tasks work together to achieve the goals of the department, you can evaluate the tasks and the information flow for potential improvements. Use the suggestions of the software technician and of your workers to spot areas that need improvement and to obtain potential solutions.

Plan a reorganization of information flow and individual work tasks, but seek critical comments from the individuals affected before the plan is put into operation. Modify your plan, as necessary, after you have evaluated the critical comments. Be prepared to make more modifications later, as you implement your plan and become familiar with its strengths and weaknesses. Use your private information system (including the organization's information system) to monitor your progress. Make sure that your changes do not cause any of the critical success factors of your department to be lowered.

Select Problems to Be Solved

After you perform the necessary surveys and solicit suggestions for improvements, you (not the software technician) will need to select the areas to be improved or problems to be solved. Do not be too ambitious in your selections since you must not expend too many personal or departmental resources. In addition, the problems that you select must have a reasonable chance of success. If you try to do too much all at once, your project will flounder and die. If you try to do too little, your accomplishments will not be significant. You need to balance your needs for success with the resources required for the project.

I recommend that your project: (1) be large enough to

be significant, (2) be small enough so that there is a reasonable expectation of success, (3) be in an area that you understand (in which you have personal expertise), and (4) be implemented in reasonably small steps.

If you try to implement too large a project or if you try to implement too much of a project all at once, the difficulty of the project will greatly increase. Implement individual parts of your project according to a flexible schedule. Build the system so that new parts can be easily inserted and so that changes to the system are easily implemented.

Determine Measurement Techniques

Before you actually implement your plans, you must make sure that you have appropriate measurement techniques for both the old and the new ways of doing things. Make sure that the measurement techniques are the same for both ways and that the techniques are either the standard ones or can be easily understood. Build the measurements into the private information system so that they are easily obtained.

Fine Tune the Private Information System

As your understanding of the problem(s) you have selected to solve evolves over time, you will need to make a number of small and a few large changes to your plans and to your private information system. These changes should be expected since you cannot be expected to understand all of the problem when you first start the project. Build your system so that these changes are relatively easy to make, and encourage an atmosphere where those associated with the project will make continual suggestions for improvement.

Prepare a Report on Your Success

During the entire project, collect documentation concerning the problem, the environment and background of the problem, solutions, successes, and failures. Use this information as the basis for your report. Remember that you have the primary responsibility to make your successes known, but make the report both clear and factual. Highlight the items that you wish to have noticed, but be subtle in your approach.

If your success is significant enough, you may be called upon to make a presentation of your findings. In both a report and a presentation you should strive for clarity and understanding, with a reasonable balance between conciseness and detail. Prepare both your report and your presentation so that they can be understood by high-level managers with different degrees of understanding and expertise. Carefully select the recipients of the original report, always including both your protector/mentor and your immediate superior. Be prepared to present details on a wide-scale implementation of your ideas, including resources needed, timetables, and costs.

12.3 Creativity

Creativity is a most difficult attribute to describe, yet it appears all around us. It usually does not require an I.Q. of 150 or more, but it does require a willingness to look at the world around and ask the question, "Is there a better way to do it?".

Creativity involves, but is not limited to: (1) an ability to see and understand that a problem exists, (2) an ability to understand the nature of a problem, (3) a willingness to try something new, and (4) the persistence to make a new approach work. It is clear that being creative and innovative cannot be taught in this book, yet it is not something you must be born with. It is a facility that you can develop as a part of your overall plan.

Try to do ordinary things in a new way, just to see what the effects are. Measure both the old way and the new way so that you can evaluate any differences. Ask yourself the questions:

1. What goal am I trying to achieve?
2. What plan do I have to achieve the goal?

3.   What am I currently doing to achieve the goal?
4.   What are the strengths and weaknesses of my approach?
5.   Is there a better approach?
6.   Can I still improve on my approach?
7.   What do I have to do to make it work?

If you can do something differently, then you are being creative. If you can do something differently and better, then you have an achievement.

I personally think that anyone can be creative since all you have to do is look at how things are done around you and then find a way to do them differently; but, remember that you don't want to do something differently just for the sake of doing it differently. You also want to do it better. Don't be afraid to experiment to some degree. Try to do things in different ways and then determine if your new techniques are better than the old ones. You will soon discover that creativity involves persistence more than anything else.

It is generally easier to find a better way to do something than it is to come up with a completely new idea; but, as you develop your creative abilities, this will probably follow also.

GLOSSARY

Access (to a File) Obtain a record from a file or place a record in a file.

Access, Direct If, in order to access a record in a file, you identify the record and the system obtains the desired record without accessing any other record in the same file, then access is called direct.

Access, Sequential If, in order to access a record in a file, you must access all records that precede it in the file, then access is called sequential.

Address The address of a record is its location in the computer or on the disk.

Analysis The act of determining the current and expected information needs and how the current information system (if any) falls short of what is needed.

Application System See: Package, application.

Byte A unit of storage in both main and secondary memory. It is roughly equivalent to one character of storage.

Column In a table or a flat file, a column is a vertical slice. For example, if a file contains employee records, with fields in the order *National Insurance number, name,* and *address,* then *National Insurance number* is the name of the first column.

Computing System The smallest computing system is a computer, secondary memory, and the associated devices for input and output. In the case of a private information system, an appropriate computing system would be a microcomputer with a hard disk, a printer, and a cable that connects the two (it is assumed here that a terminal is provided as part of the microcomputer). One might also consider the software for the computing system, such as the operating system, the instructions for use of the system, and equipment like special cabinets for the storage of disks and reports to be part of the computing system.

Conflict Requirements for a system conflict if satisfaction of one requirement implies that the other cannot be satisfied.

Contiguous Items stored in a file are contiguous if they are physically next to each other.

Criteria, Selection In many database and file management systems, one may specify which of all the records in a file are to be presented to the user. The specification that determines which records are to be selected is called the selection criteria.

Critical Success Factors   Those factors that are used by your superior to evaluate your performance. These are the areas in which you must be successful. As you implement new procedures, you must monitor the critical success factors to verify that they do not decrease.

CRT   One common type of terminal has a screen and a keyboard. The screen is a TVlike tube and displays communication to and from the computer. The screen is also called a CRT, for cathode ray tube.

Database   A database is a collection of data. If the database is maintained by a database management system, then the two words *data* and *base* are usually written as one word, *database*.

Database Management System   A database management system is a sophisticated file management system that assists in the operations of entry and storage of data and in linking or associating related records of different types together. The most common types of database management systems are hierarchical, network, and relational.

Design   The construction of a plan to meet the current and expected information needs. The plan contains specifications for files, programs, screen displays, and reports.

Disk   A disk is a device for the permanent storage of data and programs. The disk is rotated about its centre; while it is moving, information is recorded on it or read from it. Two popular types of disks are hard and floppy. A hard disk may be built into the computer disk drive or it may be removable. A floppy disk is always removable. Floppy disks represent an inexpensive alternative for the storage of data and have the capability of direct access. It takes longer to access records on a floppy disk than on a hard disk. Many different types of computers, both mainframes and micros, use hard disks as their primary type of secondary memory and also use floppy disks to facilitate the input and output of programs and data in a machine-readable form.

Duplication   One of the major problems associated with the storage of data is how to store it so that later attempts to locate it can be performed quickly. One approach to this problem is to duplicate the data so that it physically resides in different places in the computer or on the disk. This duplication may be a cause of trouble if it is not properly controlled.

Efficiency   Efficiency is the measure of how well a system works. For the most part, efficiency is measured in terms of the time that it takes to perform operations such as access to data on a disk, the execution of a program, input, and output.

Failure, Graceful   All computers have occasional problems with hardware and software. If the problem is severe enough, the computer simply stops working until you correct the problem. If the computer stops in such a manner as to help you save what you are currently doing, then we say that the failure is graceful. For example, if you are entering data into the computer and the computer asks you a question of the type, "Unable to continue. Do you wish to save the data entered during the current session?", then you are experiencing a graceful failure. If the computer merely says, "unable to continue. Process aborted.", and some or all of the entered data has been lost, then the failure is not graceful. The least graceful failure is one where the computer simply stops working, no messages are displayed by the computer, and you are left on your own. The type of failure that you encounter may be a function of either the hardware or the software, depending upon the cause of the failure.

Field A field in a computerized record corresponds to a box on a paper document. For example, a form may have a box (an area) for the last name, another box for the first name, and a box for the entire address. Thus the last name would be a field, the first name would be a field, and the entire address would be a field.

File A file is a collection of records. In most modern information systems, all of the records in a file have the same structure. The records in a file may have fixed or variable length. If the records have fixed length, all records in the file have precisely the same length. If the records have variable length, the length of individual records in a file will vary, depending upon the contents of the record. Fixed length records are currently more popular than variable length records since access to fixed length records is faster than access to variable length records.

File Management System A file management system is a software package that facilitates storage and access of data. A primitive file management system of some kind is always supplied as part of your operating system. An indexed file system is an example of a sophisticated file management system. Database management systems are specialized kinds of sophisticated file management systems.

Flexibility A system is considered flexible if it meets a variety of the user's needs. The most flexible systems can provide information so that even unanticipated needs are satisfied. For example, assume that you have information concerning each employee in your organization. The government asks you to provide a one-time report to justify your hiring and promotion policies. The information system may have no specific program to produce such a report, but you have a query facility for this purpose. You use the query facility to obtain the desired information and to print it as a report. The query facility makes this system flexible.

Friendly A system is friendly if it helps you when something goes wrong or when you do not know what to do next. For example, a system that presents you with a blank screen and then waits for you to enter something is not very friendly. In this case, when you do enter something and the only response is the message *syntax error*, then the system is really unfriendly. An example of a friendly system is one that presents you with a list of permissible operations and allows you to select from the list. In the event of an incorrect entry on your part, a friendly system will tell you what you did wrong and then suggest possible solutions to your problem.

Graphics If your computer has both the hardware and the software to help you draw pictures and graphs on the screen or on paper, it has a graphics capability. Some graphics systems allow you to produce both two- and three-dimensional pictures. Two-dimensional pictures include bar and pie charts. Three-dimensional pictures may include either line drawings (outlines) or shaded drawings. The shaded drawings may look as lifelike as a photograph. The pictures may be drawn in black and white or in colour.

Hardware The physical components of a computer are called hardware. The term *hardware* usually includes the processor, memory, terminals, and printers.

High-Level Management As used in this book, this term means anyone at the vice presidential level or higher.

Implementation The implementation of a design involves the actual construction of the files and the programs.

Incompatibility When a computer is purchased or leased, one usually also obtains a printer to go with it. If the printer simply cannot be made to operate in conjunction with the computer, then we say that the printer and computer are incompatible. In general, any two pieces of hardware or software are called incompatible if they cannot work together. If you desire to have two pieces of software, using the output from one as the input to the other, but the output from the first is not in the proper form for use by the second, they are considered to be incompatible.

Index An index file is a special file associated with a data file. The index file has two fields, a value field and a pointer (address) field. These two fields help us rapidly find records in the data file that have the specific values given in the index file. Index files are commonly used to provide direct access to files on disk.

Information System A collection of people, machines, procedures, and instructions that work together to provide information.

Interactive When a person can communicate with a computer in the form of a dialogue, the communication is called interactive.

Interface The manner or protocol in which hardware and/or software components communicate with each other is called the interface.

K A unit of measurement used for both main and secondary memory. K equals 1,024.

Keyboard The typewriterlike device that is part of a terminal.

Language, Programming A programming language is a language in which algorithms are written and which a computer can understand.

M A unit of measurement used for both main and secondary memory. M equals 1,000K, where K equals 1,024.

Mainframe A term used to describe a large computer. Unfortunately, there is no common description or definition of a large computer.

Member A component of a set in the network database management system. A set consists of an owner and zero or more members. The members of a set are related to each other by pointers.

Memory The hardware that stores data and programs. There are two common types of memory, main and secondary. Main memory is used to store programs and data while a program is running. Secondary memory is used to store data and programs over a long period of time and when the computer is shut off. Main memory is "inside" the computer, and secondary memory is usually on disk.

Mentor Someone who is willing to teach you what you need to improve your skills. More specifically someone who is willing to teach you the skills necessary to become a high-level manager.

Menu A menu is a display on the screen of the terminal of the various functions that you may select from. Menus are frequently used to make information systems friendly.

Method, Access The manufacturer of computing hardware always provides a collection of primitive techniques for accessing data. A database or file management system uses these primitive techniques as the building blocks for the construction of more sophisticated access.

Microcomputer A computer that has its central processor on one chip or integrated circuit is currently called a microcomputer.

Middle Management A middle manager is someone above the supervisory level and below the vice presidential level.

Navigate This term is used to describe how one moves from record to record in a network database system. A different technique is used to access records in each type of database and file management system. Navigation is the most complex of the various techniques.

Operating System An operating system is a program in the computer that asks you a question that is equivalent to, "What do you wish to do next?". When you respond to the question in an appropriate manner, the operating system will attempt to honour your request by carrying out the requested function.

Operator This term actually has two meanings. The person who runs a computer is called a computer operator; and the functions used to instruct the database management system to store, access, or manipulate data are also called operators.

Package, Application An application package is a program or collection of programs that has been specially written to meet your information needs.

Pointer A pointer is the address of a record.

Printer A hardware device used to produce a permanent copy of computer output. The two most popular types of printers are the dot matrix and the letter quality printers. The dot matrix printer is usually faster and cheaper than the letter quality printer. The letter quality printer produces output with quality comparable to that of a typewriter. I recommend a dot matrix printer for your private information system.

Private Information System   An information system that is written specially for individual use. It is not part of the formal (organizationally approved) information system. It may use some of the facilities of the organization's information system, but it is designed to meet specific, individual needs. Most private information systems are microcomputer based.

Processor   The part of a computer that executes (runs) a program.

Protector   Someone at a higher level of management than you are who is willing to represent your interests, and who wants to see you get ahead.

Query System   A query system is a facility that allows nonprogrammers to access data stored in the computer (or on the disk) without the help of a programmer. The request for the data is usually called a query.

Record   A record is a collection of fields all of which describe or provide attributes of a single object. A record has both a structure and a content. The structure of a record is determined by the specific fields that comprise it and, in some cases, by the ordering of the fields within the record. The content of a record provides specific information. Consider a file of applications for a job. Each application is a record for one applicant and contains information for a specific individual.

Relation   A file in a relational database management system is called a relation.

Restructure   Changing the structure of the data files or the database.

Row   A table (or flat file) is arranged as a collection of rows and columns. A row is a horizontal slice of the table and is equivalent to one record.

Set   In the network database management system, all data is arranged in sets. A set has one owner and zero or more members. Sets can be intertwined in quite complicated ways. Records may be members of more than one kind of set, owners of more than one kind of set, and owners of one kind of set while being members of another kind of set. The complexity of the set relationships makes the network database management system both powerful and complex.

Software   The programs of an information system.

Software Development System   A software development system is a collection of tools for the construction of an information system. It consists of the facilities to: (1) write programs, (2) create files in which to store data, (3) store and manipulate data, and (4) run programs. Step 4 may include the conversion of programs to machine-readable form.

Software Technician   Someone who has the training and the experience to independently (without further technical support) perform the tasks of analysis, design, and programming.

Spreadsheet   A computerized spreadsheet system allows you to enter, store, manipulate, and display data in a tabular format. Changes in data used in one part of the display are automatically proliferated to other parts of the display. Functions are usually included to facilitate the most common type of spreadsheet operations.

System   A word used to describe a collection of hardware, software, instructions, and/or people that all work together to perform a common task.

Table   A rectangular arrangement of data.

Terminal   A device that is used for two-way communication between a person and a computer.

Transaction   A document generated by an organization to record an action taken by a member of the organization is called a transaction. For example, when a salesperson records the specific items sold to a customer, a transaction has been generated (created).

Transformation   A transformation is the act of changing or manipulating data.

Transparent   An activity is called transparent if it is done in such a manner that the user is unaware of it.

User   Any member of the organization that comes into contact with the computer is called a user. There are several categories of users: those who enter data into the computer, those who operate the computer, and those who use the information provided by the computer.

Visibility   Visibility in an organization means that you have been recognized for your abilities. When problems arise and someone is needed to solve them, higher-level management thinks of you.

REFERENCES

1. Dinerstein, Nelson T. *Database and File Management Systems for the Microcomputer*. Glenview, Ill.: Scott, Foresman, 1985.
2. DeMarco, Tom. *Structured Analysis and System Specification*. Englewood Cliffs, N.J.: Prentice-Hall, 1979.

INDEX

A

Ability, problem solving, 1–6
Access, 87–89, 201, 207
 direct, 39, 88–89, 107, 207
 method, 211
 random, see Access, direct
 read only, 87
 read/write, 88
 sequential, 40, 88–89, 107, 207
 speed of, 47
 write only, 88
Accounting, 156–57
Address, 207
Advocate, see Mentor
Algorithm, 72, 139–40
Analysis, 56–65, 169–71, 207
 structured, 68, 85
Atmosphere, preparing the correct,
 131

B

Beef herd management, 160
Block, 93–94
Bypass of boss's position, 16
Byte, 207

C

Cathode ray tube (CRT), 39, 208
Checksum, 94
Code
 descriptive, 98–99
 procedural, 98–99
Coding, 73
Column, 49, 207
Communication, intelligent, 93
Compatibility, 46–47, 114
Compiler, 90–92
Computations, 99–100
Computer,
 cost of, 43–45
 types of, 43–47
Conflict, 13, 207
Contiguous, 50, 207
Coworker, 28
Creativity, see Innovation
CRT, see Cathode ray tube

D

Data, ownership of, 117–18
Data entry, 86, 96–98, 200
Data retrieval, 106–10
Database, 38, 88, 110, 119, 208
 hierarchical, 50–51
 network, 51–52
 relational, 49–50
dBASE II, 114–15
dBASE III, 114–15
Design, 65–72, 171, 208
 evolution of, 70–71
 implementation of, 66, 171–72
 preliminary, 66
 specifics of, 66, 71
 structured, 68–70
Diagram, data flow, 64, 169–71
Disk, 44–45, 111, 208
Duplicated data, 47–48, 70, 208

E

Editor, 92, 95, 110
Enemy, computer as, Preface

Energy, limit of, 9, 123
Entry, full-screen, 96
Errors, logical, 75
Evolutionary nature of
    understanding, 125–26

F

Failure, graceful, 209
Failures, record of, 30–31
Fast-food restaurant, 161
Field, 49, 110, 209
File, 68, 209
    flat, 49
Files, 87–89
    integrated, 107–9
    restructuring of, 110, 211
Fine-tuning, 48, 70, 80, 142–43,
    204
Framework, 113, 114–15
Free time, 123–25, 129, 197–98
Funds, organizational, 122

G–H

Goals, 7, 9, 125, 133–37, 193–94,
    196–97
Graphics
    capability, 48, 100–101, 111, 210
    equipment, 101–2
Hardware, 38–40, 44–47, 169, 210
High-level manager
    characteristics of, 1–6, 9, 29,
    191–92
    targeting, 178–80, 195–96

I–K–L

IBM
    AT, 44
    microcomputers, 44, 46–47, 114
    PC, 46–47
    XT, 46, 85, 201
Indexed file system, 52, 210
Information, other sources of,
    81–82
Information system
    automated, 34
    definition of, 33
    formal; see Information system,
    organizational

Information system—(cont.)
    management information
        system, 42
    manual, 34
    organizational, 2–3, 117–22,
        130, 201
    private, 4–6, 66–67, 122–23,
        130, 212
Innovation, 2, 11, 25, 129, 145–63,
    205–6
Integration of functions, 110–13
Integrity, 6, 28, 192
Interactive computing system, 210
Interpreter, 90–92
Inventory, 150–51
K, 211
Keyboard, 211
Link, 88, 109
Lotus 1-2-3, 115
Loyalty, 28

M–N–O

M, 211
Mainframe, 93, 211
Measurements, understandable,
    204
Memory, 44–45, 111, 211
Mentor, 167, 172, 179, 194–95,
    211
Menu, 211
Microcomputer, 43–47, 211
Middle manager
    abilities of, 15
    roles of, 7–16
Minicomputer, 43–47, 93
    cost of, 122
    selection of, 201–2
Modem, 46, 201
Nonprogrammer, 42
Odd ball, avoiding the appearance
    of being one, 21

P–Q

P-code, 91
Packages, integrated, 110–15
Performance, adequate, 17–19
Pharmacy, 163
Planning, 104–5, 197–205

Pointer, 51, 212
Printer, 46, 201, 212
Programming, 72–75, 95
    language, 37, 89–90, 211
    structured, 73–74
Progress, monitor, 81
Project control, 139–40
Proposal, 30, 172–73, 177–90,
    204–5
Protector, 179, 194–95, 212
Purchasing, 152–53
Query, 42, 49, 92, 119, 212

R

Real estate, 153–54
Receivables, 155–56
Record, 49, 212
Redesign, 80, 126
Redundancy, 47
Refinement, 73
Report writer, 99
Restaurant menu generator, 162
Row, 49, 212

S

Sales, 148–50
Secretary, skills of, 86
Skills, social, 85
Software, 213
    application, 37, 207
    communications, 85, 92, 95,
        201, 202
    graphics, 96, 100–102
    multi-function, 111–13
    new, 114
    other sources of, 82–83

Software development system,
    87–115, 213
    selection of, 113–15
Solution, implementation of, 23
Spreadsheet, 48, 114–15, 213
Storage, 47; see also Memory
Strategy, 191–97
System
    computing, 38, 207
    development, 125–29
    file management, 209
    operating, 37, 48, 87, 119, 211

T

Targeting an executive, 178–80
Task
    assigned, 17, 19, 21
    critical, 17
Technician, software, 53, 55–86,
    126–28, 137–39, 213
    selection of, 83–86, 168,
        199–200
Telecommunications, 93–95; see
        also Communication,
        intelligent
Telephone ordering, 157–59
Terminal, 213
Testing, 74–80, 140–42
    types of, 76–80
Tool, computer as a, Preface, 1

V–W

Viewpoint, traditional, 7–8
Visibility, Preface, 3, 19–20, 28,
    213
Word processor, 92, 110, 114
WordStar, 92, 115